Formative Assessment

Responding to Your Students

Harry Grover Tuttle

EYE ON EDUCATION
6 DEPOT WAY WEST, SUITE 106
LARCHMONT, NY 10538
(914) 833–0551
(914) 833–0761 fax
www.eyeoneducation.com

Library of Congress Cataloging-in-Publication Data
Tuttle, Harry Grover
Formative assessment : responding to your students / by Harry Grover Tuttle.
    p. cm.
    ISBN 978-1-59667-096-9
    1. Effective teaching. 2. Teacher-student relationships. 3. Academic achievement. 4. Education—Evaluation. I. Title.
LB1775.T88 2008
371.102—dc22

                                        2008028497

10 9 8 7 6 5 4 3 2 1

Also Available from EYE ON EDUCATION

Acknowledgments

I would like to thank the people who gave valuable feedback during the preparation of this book: Robert Doolittle, Linda Kurdzel, Jackie Schneider-Rivette, Alan Tuttle, Joellyn Tuttle, and Sarah Tuttle. Their constructive feedback helped me to improve the quality of this book. Reviewers Karen Bailey, Pat Murphy, Beverly Ruthven, Jason Simeroth, and Danielle Sullivan also made suggestions to help improve the original manuscript. Furthermore, I would like to thank my students, past and present, who have taught me much about the role of formative assessment in the learning process.

I especially thank my wife, Joellyn Tuttle, for her support.

I dedicate this book to Rowan, my grandson, and to other future grandchildren so that their teachers may use formative assessment to help them be successful learners.

Table of Contents

Foreword

"In years of looking at schools and jobs, I have almost never seen an ideal [feedback] system. Managers, teachers, employees, and students seldom have adequate information about how well they are performing."[1]

Thirty years ago, Thomas Gilbert, the author of the quote above summed up the principles of good feedback in his delightful and informative book *Human Competence*. In it, he catalogued the requirements of any system "designed to give maximum support to performance." The requirements involved eight steps:

1. Identify the expected accomplishments...

2. State the requirements of each accomplishment. If there is any doubt that people understand the reason why an accomplishment and its requirements are important, explain this.

3. Describe how performance will be measured and why.

4. Set exemplary standards.

5. Identify exemplary performers and any available resources that people can use to become exemplary performers.

6. Provide frequent and unequivocal feedback about how well each person is performing. This confirmation should be expressed as a comparison with an exemplary standard. Consequences of good and poor performance should also be made clear.

7. Supply as much backup information as needed to help people troubleshoot their own performance...

8. Relate various aspects of poor performance to specific remedial actions.[2]

Gilbert sardonically adds that "these steps are far too simple to be called a 'technology,' but it may be that their simplicity helps explain why they are so rarely followed."

Fast forward thirty years. Now, *formative assessment* is a phrase on every educator's lips. But we may be no closer to really understanding what formative

---

1   Gilbert, T. F. (1978). *Human Competence* (p. 178). New York: McGraw Hill.
2   Gilbert, T. F. (1978). *Human Competence* (pp. 178–9). New York: McGraw Hill.

assessment is and isn't. What is it? It is useful and timely feedback against worthy goals. What is "formative" assessment" in too many cases? Quiz results or ungraded district quarterly tests. Not the same.

One reason we rarely follow the steps outlined by Gilbert is that the phrase *formative assessment* is misleading, and it plays into a misunderstanding many teachers have. Far too many educators treat feedback as formal quiz or test results—as something one does *after* teaching and learning are over instead of seeing feedback as central to learning.[3] However, teachers err on the other side, too. Many teachers mistakenly think that making such general comments as "That was much better!" or "Good job!" is user-friendly feedback. No, this is unspecific praise, and such praise only keeps you interested; it cannot improve your performance, which is what feedback can do.

And that's why Harry Tuttle's book is so important. He provides teachers with a sound vision of formative assessment as a feedback and self-adjustment system central to instruction, and he offers a wealth of tools for ensuring that a good feedback system is set up in classrooms. Any teacher of any subject and grade level will see improved achievement and engagement from acting on Tuttle's sound advice.

Grant Wiggins

---

3   See Wiggins, G. (1998). *Educative Assessment*, San Francisco: Jossey-Bass

Preface

Numerous years ago I taught classes that each contained 58, 59, or 60 seventh-grade beginning Spanish students. I had to refocus my teaching style from being teacher-centered to student-centered in those large classes. Furthermore, I had to carefully plan each lesson to make sure that the students understood what skills they were to be learning that day, how they would be assessed, and what activities they would do to practice the learning. I had to figure out how I could present the language skills so that they could integrate those skills into conversations. My students created many of their own learning activities, particularly in the area of speaking and writing topics, which they shared with their small group and the whole class. I did not have time to assess each student on a daily basis, so I implemented many small group, peer, and self-assessments that would tell students their progress and that also included suggestions for improvement. I would monitor these assessments and offer whole-class, small-group, and individual assistance. My constructive feedback to the students needed to be easy to understand and easy to implement. Students often created quizzes for their group and assessed each other. They knew that they were partners in the learning process. Those students succeeded in being able to listen, speak, read, and write in Spanish; they constantly improved in their language use. The strategies that promoted student successful learning were a clear statement of learning goals; shared assessments; standards-based learning experiences that revealed their strengths and learning gaps; multiple forms of feedback; and time to implement the feedback to show their success. The strategies I used then are critical components of formative assessment. This past semester I taught three different subject-area classes in which I implemented a formative assessment approach in a more thorough manner.

As I have been speaking about assessment, data-driven decision making, and electronic portfolios for the past seven years, I often survey the audience on various assessment issues. I have discovered that teachers such as yourself sincerely want to help their students to be successful. Teachers understand the role of summative, end-of-the-unit, end-of-the-year, and state assessments. However, teachers often state that they do not believe they have the tools to "do" formative assessments. Teachers do observe student work in a written or oral format and teachers make decisions about instruction, but, frequently, teachers have said that they tend to make the decisions intuitively without feeling confident about defending their decisions. Teachers believe that they need more information and practical techniques to use formative assessment.

This book is a how-to book on formative assessment with many practical suggestions for the classroom teacher; the primary audience consists of classroom teachers, their principals, curriculum leaders, and preservice educators. Numerous formative assessment experts, such as Douglas Reeves, Larry Ainsworth, Rick Stiggins, Paul Black, Dylan Wiliam, W. James Popham, and Grant Wiggins, focus on national, state, or district efforts. This book supports teachers at the classroom level. As much as I have relied on the writings of formative assessment experts, I also have relied on the experiences of schools and teachers who are implementing a formative assessment approach in the classrooms.

Implementing the formative assessment process requires a change in your thinking about assessment. As you go through the book, you can select one or two strategies within each aspect that seems most appropriate for your students from the wide variety of strategies presented for each aspect of formative assessment. Also, as you read this book's chapter on formative assessment grading and think more about grading in your classroom, you may consider some changes. As you consider formative assessment, you will focus more on helping students be successful learners.

Each chapter helps you to move forward in the topic of formative assessment.

- Chapter 1 examines the strong connection between formative assessment and standards-based education. This chapter offers you many examples of sharing learning goals with your students, sharing the high quality of your expectations, and preassessing your students' present learning status.

- Chapter 2 provides suggestions for observing the present learning status of your students through what they say, do, produce, and answer on tests in terms of your learning standard.

- Chapter 3 assists you and your students in interpreting what you and they have observed so that you and they can determine the students' learning strengths and gaps.

- Chapter 4 describes various feedback techniques that allow you, the students, or students' peers to move toward closing the gap between the students' present learning and the current learning goal.

- Chapter 5 focuses on how your students can demonstrate their growth based on feedback from you, their peers, and themselves.

- Chapter 6 explains techniques for reporting your students' learning growth over time and celebrating students' learning successes in your classroom.

1

Formative Assessment: Student Response

Overview

- ◆ Setting the Stage
- ◆ Questions
- ◆ Formative Assessment Introduction
- ◆ Preassessment of Your Students
- ◆ Sharing the Learning Standards with Your Students
- ◆ Sharing the Quality of Learning with Your Students
- ◆ Summary

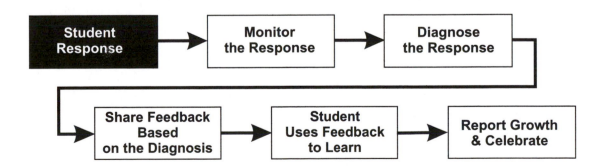

Setting the Stage

Mr. Davis, a social studies teacher at Roxboro Middle School, teaches a Civil War unit. He starts off with a lecture, has many textbook exercises for his students, sprinkles in some quizzes, and then at the end of the unit gives a final examination. Approximately 70% of his students pass the final. Meanwhile, Miss Potter, who also teaches the same social studies unit, starts off her unit with sharing the goals of the unit, explains why these goals are important to the students, gives a preassessment, shows her students samples of exemplary work to help them understand the quality she requires, does some lecturing, engages students in many in-depth activities, observes and gives feedback to each student frequently throughout the unit, has students regularly peer assess and self-assess their learning, and has a final project. Through using formative assessment, all of her students receive a proficient grade, and many receive an above-proficient grade.

Questions

- What is formative assessment?
- What are the major components of formative assessment?
- What are the similarities between formative assessment and standards-based education?
- How can you share learning goals with your students?
- How can you share the quality of the learning goals with your students?

Formative Assessment Introduction

Understand Formative Assessment and Summative Assessment Differences

Any time you assess students, you either assess in a summative or a formative way (Scriben, 1967). In a summative manner you tell students their grades or the final results; these summative assessments usually are at the end of a lesson, unit, quarter, or year. Often summative assessments are of the forced choice type such as multiple choice, and they are done during "testing" time. Conversely, in formative assessments, students do not receive a grade, but they do receive feedback that helps them to improve. You do formative assessments as part of the regular classroom learning; you embed formative assessment into classroom learning.

Summative assessments often imply an "end" to the learning; formative assessments promote "along-the-way" assessment (Tomlinson & McTighe, 2006).

Define Formative Assessment

Formative assessment refers to assessment that is specifically intended to generate feedback to improve and accelerate student learning (Sadler, 1998). You may have heard formative assessment referred to as "continuous assessment" (Erickson, 2007), "early warning assessment" (Johnson, 2005), "interactive formative assessment" (Cowie & Bell, 1999), or "dynamic assessment" (Shepard, 2000). Formative assessment occurs when you feed information back to the students in ways that enable the students to learn better, or when students can engage in a similar self-reflective process (National Center for Fair and Open Testing, 2007). Heritage (2007b) expands the concept by saying that the process involves obtaining evidence about student learning, providing feedback to students, and closing the gap between the learner's current and desired state. Formative assessment is not a specific type of assessment, rather it is the manner in which the assessment is used (Afflerbach 2005). Popham (2008) emphasizes that formative assessment is a process. Figure 1.2 illustrates the aspects of formative assessment.

Figure 1.1. Formative Assessment Process

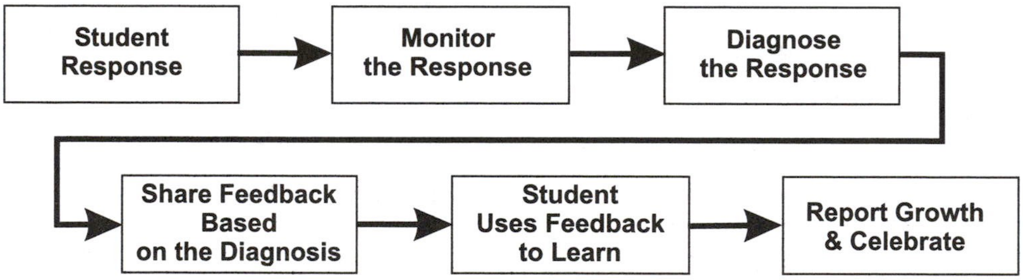

Incorporate Formative Assessments into the Bigger Assessment Picture

State tests, course finals, quarterly benchmarks, and unit tests are important because they summarize your students' past learning; however, they do not help the students improve on a regular weekly basis as classroom formative assessments do. These summative assessments reveal what was learned, but they do not provide specific suggestions for the students to improve. When you use formative assessments you identify the present status of the students in terms of the learning standard, diagnose what to do to assist them, provide feedback, allow students to make the changes, and celebrate their learning successes. The following visual demonstrate the bigger picture of assessment.

Figure 1.2. Big Assessment Picture

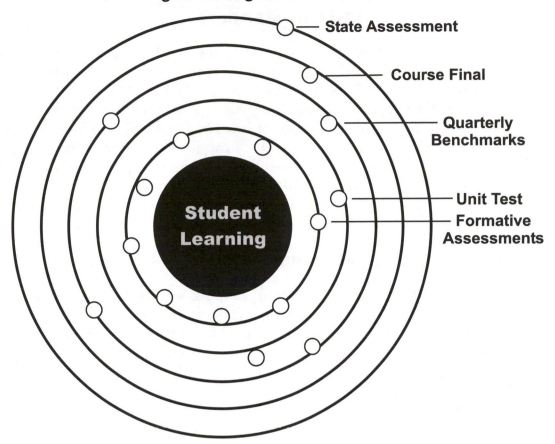

Learn the Advantages of Formative Assessment

Why would you want to use formative assessment? When teachers use formative assessment, students can learn in six to seven months what will normally take a school year to learn (Leahy, Lyon, Thompson, & Wiliam, 2005). Furthermore, Ainsworth and Viegut (2006, p. 23) explain that when you use formative assessment, you are better able to: determine what standards students already know and to what degree; decide what changes in instruction to make so that all students succeed; create appropriate lessons, activities, and groupings; and inform students about their progress to help them set goals. Also, formative feedback is the most powerful single moderator in the enhancement of achievement (Hattie, 1998). In addition, the research of Black and Wiliam (1998) emphasize that this approach works extremely well with at-risk students.

Connect Formative Assessment Process and the Standards

Formative assessment focuses on helping the teacher understand "how" students can improve in their learning so that they can be proficient. Standards-based education has been focused on "what" the students learn; standards refer to the specific learning designated by national educational organizations, state departments of education, or local school districts. Once you help students to know what they are to learn, they can focus on how to learn it well. Standards-based education and a formative assessment approach share many common characteristics. When standards-based education and a formative assessment approach are combined, teachers like you have a powerful learning tool.

Identify Formative Assessment Strategies

The purpose of formative assessment, helping students improve in their learning, is a simple concept, yet this simple concept encompasses many distinct strategies. Many educators (Black & Wiliam, 1998; Sadler, 1998b; Stiggins, 2007; Heritage, 2007a) have identified what constitutes formative assessment.

- Preassessing students
- Sharing learning goals with students
- Sharing or co-creating of learning criteria with students
- Employing quality classroom discourse and questioning
- Using rich and challenging tasks that elicit students' responses
- Identifying the gap between where the students are now and the desired standard goal
- Providing feedback that helps students identify how to improve
- Using self-assessment and peer assessment
- Providing students with opportunities to close the gap between current and desired performance
- Celebrating learning progressions

This formative assessment listing looks very similar to a standards-based learning chart designed by O'Shea (2006, pp. 98–100) as shown in Figure 1.3 where the standard component is on the left and the formative assessment is on the right.

Figure 1.3. Standards-Based Learning

Components*	In a formative assessment approach and a standards-based lesson
Edits the chosen standard to select a key goal for the unit. Paraphrases it in the student's language.	♦ Tells the students the standard in their language. ♦ Has posted the standard and refers to it throughout the unit.
Plans for assessments on the standard before, during, and after the unit.	♦ Preassesses students to determine their present status in the standard. ♦ Informs students of the high level of expectation in the standard, and shows them exemplars. ♦ Informs students of the format of assessments. ♦ Frequently gives formative standards-based assessments and analyzes the results. ♦ Gives a post-assessment that represents the highest thinking level of the standard.
Develops performance tasks.	♦ Tells students how in-class tasks, homework, and projects advance them in the standard. ♦ Assigns performance tasks that clearly demonstrate the standard. ♦ Observes the results of each performance task to adjust instruction.
Scaffolds the performance tasks.	♦ Scaffolds through using various sequential performance tasks to help all students climb the cognitive ladder in the standard.
Incorporates the standard's key vocabulary throughout the unit.	♦ Includes key vocabulary in teaching and requires it in students' oral, visual, and written responses.

*From *Standards to Success* (pp. 98–100), by M. R. O'Shea, 2006, Alexandria, VA: Association for Supervision and Curriculum Development.

In addition, Reif's (2004) explanation of standards-based learning mirrors a description of formative assessment. Curriculum and instruction are not based on a textbook but on the standards that all students are to meet through differentiated instruction. Also, assessments are not used to determine a grade but to inform students of expectations and achievements. In the same manner, student feedback is much more than just a letter grade; student feedback focuses on progress toward meeting the standards. Students do more than focus on the current activity; they describe where they are in the learning progress and know what they can do to achieve the learning goals. Teachers in teams collaboratively assess students' work and decide how to improve the students' performance

Preassessment of Your Students

Once you have identified the standard and its highest quality level, create a preassessment (pretest, diagnostic tests, or baseline data test). The preassessment allows you to monitor and adjust instruction. Do you start your class within the first few weeks of the year with a diagnostic test of where the students are in terms of the skills and knowledge that they need for your class so you can create differentiated instruction for the learning success of all students (Tomlinson & McTighe, 2006)? Stronge's (2002) research reveals that teachers in schools with high achievement rates use preassessment to support targeted teaching. Figure 1.4 represents a formative assessment view of the percentage of assessments done at different parts of the unit (Tuttle, 2007e).

Figure 1.4. Unit Assessment Percents

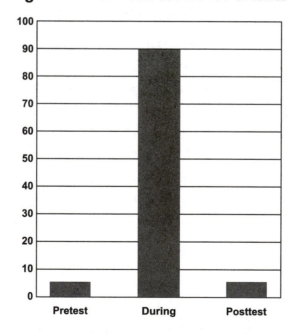

If your diagnostic test does not cover the whole year, does it cover a truly representative part of the course? A high school business teacher, Mr. Barrera, has his students write a business application letter during the second class. He quickly determines which parts of a business letter the students can do already and which the students need improvement in. After looking at this short diagnostic test, he has a solid idea of what he can do to improve student learning in the course and how to modify the upcoming unit.

Your students take the pretest several weeks before the unit so that you have adequate planning time to modify the unit. These pretests do not have to be complex. They will assess the whole standard or the goals (major components of the standard) at its highest level of thinking, and they will assess the comprehensive nature and the in-depth nature of the standard. A pretest covers one of many different aspects (Tuttle, 2007c):

- All the year's key concepts: A science teacher has developed two questions for each of the key goals that she covers during the year. She gives this pretest at the beginning of the year to have a baseline for all her students. Another science teacher selects standards-based questions from the standards testing program, has the students take the online assessment, and studies the results.

- Content on the state assessment: A Spanish teacher may give the students the previous year's state assessment during the second week of the school year to see what skills and knowledge the students presently possess.

- Overarching skills or concepts: An English teacher uses a reading comprehension pretest at the beginning of the year to determine how well the students comprehend reading materials. The English teacher realizes that if students do not have a high degree of reading comprehension, they will not do well in the course.

- Several standards goals found in a unit: A math teacher pulls out four questions that are the most difficult and that represent different standards goals from the unit; she asks her students to solve these problems.

- A specific goal within a unit: Within a big government and civics unit, a social studies teacher creates several pretests, each one focusing on a different goal, such as the purpose of the Constitution, the three branches of government, and the Bills of Rights in daily life. As the students finish one section of the unit, they have a pretest on the next section.

- Misconceptions: As a science teacher plans the unit, he thinks about all the misconceptions that previous students have displayed about this standard, and he examines the results from previous year's tests. He pinpoints the difficulties that students had. He writes a pretest to assess his present students for these misconceptions.

- Performance tasks: A Mandarin language teacher assesses at the highest level and in the same way that the state assessments evaluates the speaking skill. She has her students talk about a topic such as hobbies to see if they can say 10 coherent sentences within a short time period.

♦ Students' self-assessment: Students are given a list of goals or performance tasks, and they check off which ones they are very confident that they can do in an elementary music course. Although this a perception pretest, it helps the students reflect on their own skills and knowledge and provides the teacher a view of what they feel are their strengths and learning gaps (Tomlinson & McTighe, 2006).

In addition to giving the preassessment, you will want to be able to analyze the results. For example, Mr. Barrera in his global studies class created an analytic rubric (a rubric in which each critical component is rated individually); he records the results for each part of the rubric in a spreadsheet. He can easily see the class strengths and learning gaps as well as individual's results. He focuses on closing the gap and providing enrichment for those who are already proficient. Meanwhile, Ms. Ariani has her global studies students take an online preassessment on the major geographic, economic, religious, and cultural aspects of the countries she will cover in the next unit. The online program provides her with an analysis of each question so that she can fine-tune her upcoming unit to maximize student learning through differentiated instruction (Tuttle, 2007e, 2007f).

Sharing the Learning Standards with Your Students

Once your district, school, or team has selected the standards from national educational organizations, state education departments, or your local school district for your subject area, and you have unpacked those standards (deciding what students will know or be able to do at the end of the unit), you have the responsibility of communicating those standards to the students. As you and your team try to better understand the standard, you analyze the verbs used in the standard to understand what students are expected to do or know. Once you and the students know where they are going academically, you and they can provide better feedback to grow in that learning. Standards make a hidden learning curriculum into an explicit and overt one for the students. Standards serve as a road map for the students' learning (Heritage, 2007a). However, before you share the standard and its goals, you will want to make sure that the students can understand the standard.

Reword the Standards

You may reword the standards for your students so that the standards are stated in student-friendly language. When you translate the standards, you come to better understand what the standard expects. You study the performance standards and then reword them into "I can" statements that students and parents can understand. For example, the National Geography Standard 2 of "how to use mental maps to organize information about people, places, and environments in a spatial context" becomes rewritten into the elementary Hawaii content standard of "I can name and locate on a map the seven continents, four oceans, the equator, North Pole, South Pole, Northern Hemisphere, and Southern Hemisphere" (Hawaii Geographic Alliance, 2006).

In another strategy, you find the equivalent of your state standard in another state that has student-friendly language instead of the teacher language used in most state standards. A New York State Education Department's (n.d.) state version of Standard 2: World History Key Idea 1 is "the study of world history requires an understanding of world cultures and civilizations, including an analysis of important ideas, social and cultural values, beliefs, and traditions." You and your high school students can compare that standard's wording to the South Carolina's family friendly list of learning, which explains what the students will be learning for 10th grade social studies: "Compare the origins and characteristics of the Mayan, Aztecan, and Incan civilizations" (South Carolina Education Oversight Committee, 2007). As you and your students look at standards written in student friendly language, you all can better understand them.

Because students are the ones who are to demonstrate their success in the standard, they can rewrite the standard in their own words. They do this individually, in small groups, or as a whole class. You facilitate their analyzing and interpreting of the standard into the student's own words. Through your facilitating questions, the students can go from the top level "What does this standard want you to be able to do or know?" to "What skills or knowledge do you have to demonstrate to be successful?" One strategy is to have the students identify the key verbs in the standard and then to rewrite these verbs into equivalent-level thinking verbs. The students' discussion will quickly reveal much about their understanding of this standard.

By asking the students a situational question, you can help elicit a standard from them. As you ask them the situational question of, "What would our life be like without electricity?," you draw out from them the social studies standard about changes over time. By using a know, want to know, and learned (KWL) chart for a given topic in your class, the topic becomes the starting point for the classroom learning. As an elementary science teacher, you ask your students to make a KWL chart about plants as you help them formulate questions about what all living things need.

Post the Standards

Your classroom instruction does not become a standards-based formative assessment approach simply by posting the standards in your room. Posting the standard becomes effective when you enlarge the standards to list the critical key goals for your class. For example, as an Arizona world language teacher, you list the standard and the major goals that you have for the Communication Standard 1.2 and indicate with an arrow which specific goal the students will be developing in this class (State Education Department of Arizona, n.d.) as in Figure 1.5.

Figure 1.5. Cummunication Standard and Goals

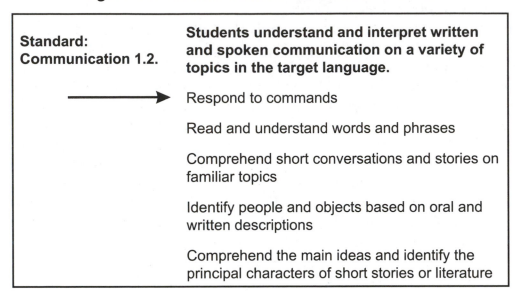

For this language goal, you start off each class by asking the students to state the day's learning goal and to paraphrase it in their own words.

Change Your Teacher Talk and Your Students' Talk to Be Standards Based

When you teach in a formative assessment approach and standards-based approach, you no longer talk about the learning activity, but you change your talk to focus on the standard's learning purpose for any lesson or unit. As a standards-based English teacher, you will not say "We are going to spend the next two weeks reading Steinbeck's *Of Mice and Men*," which is an activity. Instead you say, "We will be developing your skills in comparing and contrasting, which is an important part of Standard 3: Critical Analysis. By the end of this unit, you will be able to compare and contrast the different themes in Steinbeck's *Of Mice and Men*." Those two different verbal introductions to the unit convey very different meanings to the students about what they are expected to learn. The first statement tells the students nothing about what they are to learn, it just tells the students that they will be reading, the context of their learning. The second statement clearly explains what the students are expected to do at the end and what learning context (the novel) they will use.

In a formative assessment approach, you use statements such as "We are learning to..." when you refer to the standard's purpose of activity. Likewise, you use statements such as "Remember to...." when you refer to success criteria. Immediately before the students start a learning task, you can ask "So what do you need to remember to do to... (achieve the standard)?" You word process their responses so they can use them as criteria for their own self-assessment and for feedback. You can post these in the room and give each student a copy of the criteria written in their own words (Primary National Strategy, 2004, p. 4).

Not only does your classroom teacher-talk change, but even more importantly, students classroom talk changes to reflect their understanding of the learning goals expected of them. For example, frequently during your middle school math lesson based on the Idaho math standards, you ask "What are we learning today?," and you expect to hear a paraphrase of the standard such as "We are evaluating simple algebraic expressions using substitutions." (Idaho State Department of Education, 2007). The students' answers indicate that they are focused on the standard and not just on the activity. Their classroom talk centers on the standard.

Modify Daily Agendas to Become Learning Agendas

Likewise, instead of giving the daily agenda that lists that day's activities, state the daily agenda by listing the learning goals that you want the students to successfully learn or do. If you write on the chalkboard, blog, or class website, "Finish reading Chapter 2 and answer the end of the chapter questions," the students do not know what you expect them to learn; they only know what they are to do. Your agenda is an activity, not a learning goal. The students will only know when they are done answering the questions but not what they are to learn from the experience. If you write, "After reading the chapter, contrast pre-Revolutionary life to post-Revolutionary life in five ways," then the students have a specific purpose that helps them work toward achieving the social studies standard. Students know what they are to learn from reading. As they read, they will be focused on the post-Revolutionary life and trying to identify differences with the pre-Revolutionary life. Here are several examples of the difference between non–standards-based daily agendas and formative assessment daily learning agendas as shown in Figure 1.6.

Figure 1.6. Non-Standard to Formative Agenda

Non–Standards-Based Daily Agenda	Formative Assessment Daily Learning Agenda
Social studies: Finish reading Chapter 2	Contrast pre-Revolutionary life to post-Revolutionary in five ways in a chart based on your readings
Math: Do problems	Explore multiple ways of creating numbers such as 100
Mandarin language: Restaurant words	Role-play a conversation with a waiter about five problems in the restaurant

Begin and End the Class with the Standard

Each day you can start your class with a review of the standard and how that translates into your daily lesson. You can either employ the standard-to-the-class approach or the standard-skills-mastery approach. In the standard-to-the-class approach, show the students the path from the general outcome to the specific learning goal for the day. When students have a firm orientation as to where they are to end up in the unit, they better self-assess how far they have progressed. For example, as a high school business teacher, you use the following standard from the National Business Education Association (2001):

> Foundation of Communication Standard I: Communicate in a clear, courteous, concise, and correct manner on personal and professional levels:
>
>> Major goal: Produce clear and concise computer-generated professional letters.
>>
>> Goal: Produce clear and concise computer-generated direct request letters.
>>
>> Specific learning goal: Produce clear and concise computer-generated direct request order letters.
>>
>> Assessment: Write a direct-request order letter and check it against an exemplar.

In the standards-skill-mastery approach, you review those goals or those building blocks (components of each goal) for which the students have already shown proficiency. When students see their successes, they are motivated to continue in their learning. When you end each class with a review and affirmation of the major goals for the standard, you help students realize how much progress they have made each day. For example, a high school business teacher lists the following:

Foundation of Communication Standard I: Communicate in a clear, courteous, concise, and correct manner on personal and professional levels.

Goal: Produce clear and concise computer-generated direct request letters.

Skills presently mastered by the class:

- Can use a block style
- Can include all the necessary parts of the letter (return address, your address, salutation, etc.)
- Can identify the request letter body general format of: first paragraph, front-load the message; second paragraph, give details; and third paragraph, specify action date
- Can identify the specific items needed in the front-load section, the detail sections, and the specific action for an order letter

Label Each Assignment as to the Specific Critical Goal of the Standard

Imagine how much more focused the students will be about the learning goal if every time you give an in-class assignment, homework, or a project, you label the precise standard and critical goal for the classroom learning. Within a lesson and within a unit, focus on the same standard and the same goal so you can easily copy that standard goal from your word processor to any assignment. The part of the standard that will vary is the particular learning goal that the students achieve as you help them to quickly move from memorization up to higher levels of thinking. Students have both a telescopic view of the standard and a microscopic view of the particular learning task (standards-based activity) when you include both the standard and the particular learning task. For example, as a science teacher using the Kansas State Education Department's (n.d.) standard for physical science, you write on the top of a worksheet:

Standard 2: Physical science: You will increase your understanding of the properties of objects and materials that you encounter on a daily basis. You will compare, describe, sort, and classify these materials by observable properties.

Topic: States of water

Learning task: Observe water going from a frozen cube, to water, and to vapor

Sharing the Quality of Learning

Once students know what they are to learn or do, they want to know how well they are to learn it or the quality of learning you expect of them. Just as you carefully selected those standards that your students are to learn, you will examine the standard and the state assessment to identify the high level of quality that the standard requires. During this analysis, you might consider studying the verbs in the standard that indicate how well students are to do or know a particular learning. You can demonstrate this quality in many ways as described in the following sections.

Find or Create Exemplars to Show the Class the High Expectation Level for the Standard

An *exemplar,* a model piece of work, clearly shows an above-proficient demonstration of the standard. It exemplifies both the in-depth and comprehensive nature of the learning. Do not identify an assignment as exemplary for other than standards-based reasons. If you select an inferior work to motivate a particular student, then you have lowered the high expectations for the whole class. Being the cutest, the most decorative, the longest, the neatest, or the most glitzy does not make an activity an exemplar; only directly showing the standard at its highest level makes it an exemplar.

If you have taught the standard previously, you may have saved some student exemplars that show a mastery of the standard at its highest level of thinking. If so, show the class these exemplars at the beginning of the lesson or unit. Emphasize how these exemplars proficiently demonstrate the standard or have the students explain why these are exemplars. If you do not have exemplars from past years, ask your colleagues in your building or district, ask colleagues in the professional organizations to which you belong, or search the Internet for exemplars from other teachers or organizations. Sometimes you will find something that comes close to being exemplary and then you can modify it to be of the high quality you expect in the standard. Sometimes I have taken parts from the work of several students and put those selected parts together to create a single exemplar. If you cannot find an exemplar, then create one. Creating the exemplar may take time, but your exemplar will precisely demonstrate the standard for the students. An additional benefit of your creating the exemplar is you also identify the exact skills the students will be required to use for above-proficient standard work. Your team might help you in creating exemplars that all of you can use. For example, your high school business team can create a model business letter for ordering supplies. Students identify all the parts that are contained in the exemplar so that they know what to include in their letters.

When students see several different exemplars for the same standard, they realize that the standard becomes the important focus, not the manner in which they present the standard learning. They also see that each exemplar has the same high level of thinking (Clarke, 2005). If you have a digital camera, you can take pictures of exemplars that students produce in the classroom and use those exemplars to help other students in their learning journey.

In your classroom post the exemplar and then have a sheet that explains what makes it an exemplar. Your sheet identifies the standard, its critical goal, the performance tasks demonstrated, and the highest level of thinking required by that standard. For example, as an art teacher, have your students focus on photography to create an original work of art (California State Board of Education, 2007). Post this exemplar explanation (Figure 1.7) in your room or to your class blog (a web-based discussion area) or website so that students can refer to it throughout the unit. Ask students to compare their work to the exemplar and note any differences.

Figure 1.7. Art Exemplar Explanation

California Visual and Performing Arts Standard 2: Creative Expression

Students apply artistic processes and skills, using a variety of media to communicate meaning and intent in original works of art.

Communication and Expression through Original Works of Art

2.6: Create an original work of art, using film, photography, computer graphics, or video.

Exemplar:
A photograph of a couple sitting in a gorge

This is an exemplar because it

♦ Uses the rule of thirds to place the couple in the intersection of horizontal and vertical thirds.

♦ Uses prospective. Has the couple looking at the far away trees that the gorge narrows into.

♦ Uses color contrast. Contrasts the couple's bright clothing colors with the earth tones of the gorge.

Reeves (2006) advocates that schools and classrooms have a wall of fame where students' exemplary work (the fame) can be posted so that all students know that they can succeed in learning the standard. In addition, the students see what other students have done to succeed. These exemplars serve as formative learning guides for the students.

Learn to Identify Quality Standard Work through the Use of Assessment Tools

You can help your students to not only know what they are to learn but also understand the high quality that you expect of them through the use of various assessment tools such as rubrics (assess explicitly stated criteria for student work), rating scales (rate specified learning on a number scale such as 1–10), checklists (check off existing learning from a list), and success criteria (identify demonstrated behaviors from a listing of those critical behaviors or traits for this particular learning). The quality can be measured by the level of thinking required. Such assessment tools empower students to peer assess and self-assess themselves.

The Nebraska Department of Education (2007) has identified various levels of quality learning involved in a social studies "the causes and effects of a war" learning goal:

Beginning: Lists or names the causes of the war

Progressing: Prioritizes the causes of the war

Proficient: Indicates the cause and the effects of the war

Advanced: Compares and contrasts the cause and effect of one conflict to a different conflict

With these levels, you and your students see the progress of learning from a beginning level to an advanced level. Your school district, school, or teams identify the learning levels for the major learning goals and share these with the students so they understand the level expected of them.

You can create your own assessment tool or obtain one from a colleague. To find a rubric online, search for your learning goal +rubric, for example, conflict plus rubric or "Civil War" +rubric. As you look at a preexisting assessment tool such as an online rubric, verify that the rubric assesses your specific standard and assesses it at its highest level. Unfortunately some web-based rubric generators do not contain levels of performance or quality that explain the difference in quality levels such as those between advanced, proficient, growing, and starting in the standard:

Advanced—Has a complete explanation (or shows complete understanding)

Proficient—Adequately explains the information

Growing—Has some of the information

Starting—Has a little of the information

How do these statements help students who received a starting designation? Even if the rubric specifies a number of sentences for each level, students still do not understand the quality difference because more sentences does not necessarily mean more quality. When the rubric information is so vague, then the students do not have a formative path to follow for success. Such rubrics are not helpful in a formative assessment approach.

Furthermore, many rubrics do not distinguish between which categories (criteria or dimensions) are critical and which are less critical. For example, on the New York State Comprehensive Writing Assessment (New York State Education Department, 2007), the content that the students write and the grammar conventions that they use are each given the same scoring weight. A student may not communicate the prescribed content but still score high on the rubric because the rubric uses a holistic grading system in which the overall score is determined by which category has the most mini-scores.

The three questions proposed by Sadler (1998) can help evaluate any assessment tool:

- Does it clearly indicate the standard and the high quality expected for the standard?

- Does it clearly indicate to the student how the student's present performance compares to this standard and quality?

- Does it clearly indicate to the student how to close the gap between where the student is now in the learning progression and the expected high quality of the standard?

Guide your students in better understanding the quality desired in a preexisting assessment tool, such as a teacher rubric, or through their creating their own assessment tool. Some strategies are:

- Model the feedback process based on a rubric as you do a think-aloud as a student would for a sample work (Clarke, 2005). Explain aloud how you assess the work as you go through each part of the rubric.

- Students paraphrase the assessment tool in pairs and mutually decide on what the individual parts of the rubric means.

- Students, individually, and then as a whole class, analyze previous students' work according to a standards-based assessment tool. You encourage a discussion over what the rubric really requires and where evidence of this is found in the student's work. Furthermore, you make sure that when the students talk about a piece of work, they use the standard's vocabulary found in the scoring tool as the basis for their feedback to others.

- The students can go through the rubric line by line as they apply it to a sample work. They highlight each rubric key word in a specific color and then highlight evidence of that key word in the student's work in the same color. Next they indicate what improvements the student can do to demonstrate the standard at a proficient level.

- Students analyze two or more exemplary products with the assessment tool to see how quality work can be done in various forms.

- Students rate several examples of students' work by using an assessment tool to improve their ability to recognize high-quality standards-based student work (Reeves, 2004). As students become more discriminating, they can be given several pieces of students' work that are on the border of two levels such as proficient and above-proficient.

- When students are co-creators of a rubric, they are more invested in the criteria, and they come to understand the standard better (Stiggins, 2007a). You can show them several pieces of work, have them decide on the differences, and have them use those differences to create a rubric for a proficient piece of work. Then you have the class try out the rubric by assessing several pieces of work.

Summary

- Formative assessment refers to the monitoring, diagnosing, and giving feedback that helps students to improve their learning in the current learning standard.

- Formative assessment moves students forward in their learning, whereas summative assessment tells them what their learning was.

- Formative assessment and standards-based education share many common characteristics. Standards-based education focuses more on "what" the students are to learn, whereas formative assessment focuses more on "how" to help the learners be successful.

- You can share the learning goals with your students in many different ways so that they are sure of the ending targets; therefore, they can focus their efforts.

- Likewise, you can help the students understand the quality expected of them in their learning through assessment tools such as rubrics, rating scales, checklists, and exemplars. They can generate their own quality lists so that they can achieve the high level expected of them.

- By preassessing your students before instruction, you know the entering learning status of your students and therefore, you can better differentiate instruction to promote better learning.

2

Formative Assessment: Monitoring

Overview
- Setting the Stage
- Questions
- Introduction
- Monitoring Student Learning through What They Say, Do, Produce, and Answer on Tests
- Small Group, Peer, and Self-Monitoring
- Recording the Observations
- Summary

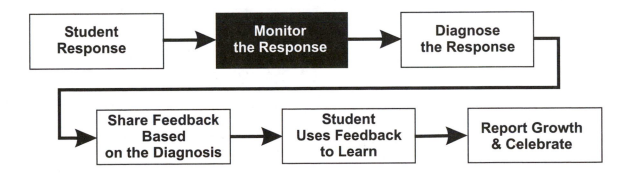

Setting the Stage

After a whole-group math instruction, Miss Burke observes as Grover uses his manipulatives to express various ways of forming 100. She notices that several of his groupings do not equal 100. Without her careful monitoring, she cannot move on to diagnosis and formative feedback to help Grover improve in his math.

Question

♦ What are formative assessment strategies that monitor where the students are in the learning process?

♦ How can teachers and students record that information?

Introduction

Because the goal of formative assessment focuses on improving student learning in the specified learning goal, the first step involves eliciting student responses to reveal student thinking (Black & Wiliam, 1998; Stronge, 2002). You need evidence of what the students know and do not know. The teaching and learning process depends on students responding so that you can determine the next instructional strategy for the students' success. The following visual metaphors (Figure 2.1) depict the importance of observing student responses.

Figure 2.1. Importance of Student Responses

Classroom learning is in total darkness until students brighten it with their responses.

We **cannot proceed** in classroom instruction until students give some signal of their learning.

To monitor (observe) students you need to step outside of the stream of classroom interaction long enough to observe precisely what the students are doing in the class. If the class rushes by like a flood, then you probably do not notice what is happening. You can build in mini-floodgates by increasing student activities such as wait time, think-pair-share, journal writing, and small group, pair, and individual activities that allow you to stop the class flow long enough to capture the students' learning. By building in observation time, you can see the tip of students' learning; Joyce and Williamson use an iceberg metaphor to visualize how little of students' thinking shows above the surface while the vast majority of their thinking hides far below the surface (Butler & Munn, 2006).

When you engage your students in higher-level thinking activities as indicated by Bloom's taxonomy, you observe their in-depth and comprehensive thinking about the standard. Their high level thinking allows you to see more of their thinking. If students work on Bloom's (1956) knowledge or memorization level, then you have very little to see. You can increase what you see about your students' thinking by having them work collaboratively on assignments, perform authentic tasks, undertake complex tasks, and design and implement community-related tasks. Also, you see more of their thinking when they reflect on the work of others and their own work.

During this phase of the formative assessment cycle, you obtain evidence, observing what the students say, do, produce, or answer on tests. Monitoring also may be referred to as "dipsticking" (Hunter, 1976) and as a "learning probe" (Cotton, 1988). When you monitor, you observe how the students are demonstrating their standard's learning. NASA sends out probes to find information that it analyzes at a later time just as you send out learning probes in your classroom.

Monitoring Student Learning through What They Say, Do, Produce, and Answer on Tests

When you monitor or observe students, you are looking at what learners do in four areas (Butler & Munn, 2006; Hall & Burke, 2003). You observe for what the students

- ◆ say

- ◆ do (their actions)

- ◆ produce (their work)

- ◆ answer on tests

You can observe students based on embedded, planned for, or spontaneous assessments (Heritage 2007a). In curriculum-embedded assessments, select key points during the learning process that your students do on a regularly scheduled basis, such as a weekly science log. In the planned for or structured interactions, plan out, prior to class, activities or questions that will elicit student thinking during that class. The most frequently occurring of all assessments are the spontaneous or on-the-fly ones that take place during the course of the lesson as you listen to a group discussion, hear a science misconception, or respond to a student's question.

The following sections provide an overview of each observation area, some general categories, and a few specific examples. Although the observation classroom examples focus on monitoring, many also illustrate diagnosing, giving feedback, and students showing success in their learning.

Observe for What Students Say

When students are silent, they present a blank screen. You cannot help the students because you do not know what the students are thinking. You probably do not have psychic abilities to divine a students' thinking, but you do have the power to change the way in which you ask questions to invite more of a response, to structure learning experiences that invite student comment, and to create more dialogue with students.

Question

Questions are most valuable when students respond, correctly or incorrectly, because their responses encourage student engagement, demonstrate understanding or misconceptions, and further the discussion (Stronge, 2002). However, "a mistake is a better indicator of successful mathematical activity than a correct answer. Whereas pupils who know the correct answer may simply be repeating what they have been told, pupils who make a mistake have often worked this out through mathematical activity" (Hodgen & Marshall, 2005, p. 170).

You might have discovered that some of your questions receive very little response. Madeline Hunter (1982), the originator of "checking for understanding," has identified three common types of ineffective questions that some teachers use in checking for understanding:

1. "O.K.?" The question assumes that student silence translates as "OK" and that they understand the learning goal.

2. "You all understand, don't you?" or "You don't have any questions, do you?" Few students are willing to publicly admit they do not understand. In fact, most students work hard to keep their teacher from discovering that they do not know or cannot do something. Yet one of the most important pieces of information that teachers can have is the knowledge that students have not yet acquired the necessary understanding.

3. "Now does anyone have a question?" Too often such a question carries the implication that "If you do have questions, you obviously were not listening or you are not very bright." (pp. 59–62)

Discuss

A dramatic way to increase how much you can see of students' thinking through classroom discussion involves changing your questions from closed-ended (factual, one-word answers) to open-ended (thoughtful, answers of multiple sentences) as Figure 2.2 illustrates.

Figure 2.2. Closed-Ended Versus Open-Ended Questions

Closed-ended questions like:	Open-ended questions like:
When did…?	How do you explain…?
Who invented…?	How well did they succeed?
What are the five steps…?	Why did this reaction happen?
Where is…?	What might happen next…?
Which is bigger?	What do you think could?
	What are some possible solutions to…?
	Which may be a better beginning?

When you rephrase a question into an agree–disagree statement, students think more and then reveal more of their thinking. Clarke (2005) transforms an original recall question of "Which drugs are bad for you?" into the reframed question of "All drugs are bad for you. Do you agree or disagree and why?" (p. 71).

You may have found that pauses in the classroom discussion often lead to deeper insights as the students have more time to process the information. When students are given wait time such as five seconds to think before they answer, they answer more often and answer in more complete thoughts (Black & Wiliam, 1998; Stronge, 2002). This wait time can be extended to five seconds after an answer, a teacher response, and a student response according to Marzano (2007). Each wait time allows the students to think through the issue. The wait time incorporates a "no-hands up, wait until you are called on" questioning process. The following illustrates wait time in a middle school social studies class that is exploring immigration:

Miss Nave: What might be some of the experiences that the immigrants coming to the United States go through? (Waits five seconds)

Miss Nave: Kayla? (Waits five seconds)

Kayla: They are scared. (Miss Nave begins to wait five seconds.)

Kayla: (she adds after three seconds) since they do not speak English. (Waits five seconds.)

Miss Nave: Why would not speaking English make them scared? (Waits five seconds.)

Kayla: They do not know how to ask for food or ask for a place to sleep.

Elicit Responses from Class Discussion Questions

Some of your questions can get more student responses than others. Lipton and Wellman (1998) offer some suggestions for making questions more inviting to answer.

1. Invitation to think, which consists of your use of:

    ■ Having an approachable voice. Raise your voice at the end to indicate a question.

    ■ Using plural forms. Ask "What are some reasons for...?" instead of "What is a reason for...?" Plural forms indicate there are multiple right answers and, therefore, invite the student to respond.

    ■ Using exploratory language. Use "might," "some," and "could" such as "What might be the causes of...?" or "What are some possible explanations?" that indicate multiple possible responses.

    ■ Using open-ended forms. Use question words and phrases like "How...?, "Why...," and "What are some other...?" that encourage students to widen their thinking.

    ■ Starting with positive preliminary statements. Ask "As you examine the data table, what are some of the details you are noticing?" Or "Reflect for a minute on the following—and compare your thinking today to your thinking about this topic last week. What are some similarities and differences that are emerging?"

    ■ Avoiding starters like "Have you...?, "Can you...?" , "Did you...?," or "Who knows..?"

2. Cognition. Select thinking verbs that represent Bloom's level of thinking that you expect of the students such as synthesis (create, design, formulate, hypothesize) or evaluating (recommend, prioritize, accept/reject, justify). You use these verbs in your statements and questions such as "What might be some ways to design...?"

3. Topic. Have a topic which invites diverse thinking and multiple perspectives. For example, you may have your students investigate the exploration of Mexico from the viewpoint of the Spanish government, the Spanish Catholic church, the conquistadors, and the native Mexican people. (p. 48)

You can assess students' learning though listening to your students. Some randomly arranged examples are shown in Figure 2.3.

Figure 2.3. Monitor What Students Say

_____	Class discussion	_____	Small group talk
_____	Debate	_____	Play/drama
_____	Oral presentations	_____	Reciting a poem/speech
_____	Story/event retelling	_____	Panel discussion
_____	Agree/disagree and why	_____	Music
_____	Choral readings	_____	Interviews
_____	Think-Pair-Share	_____	Think alouds
_____	You're the judge	_____	Answer specific
_____	Ask a question	_____	Continuum lines/corners' discussions
_____	Make a statement	_____	Podcast
_____	Radio Show	_____	Read alouds
_____	Other _____	_____	Other _____

The following classroom activities represent a few examples of observation through what students say:

Ask Questions Using Cards, Fingers, and Hand-Held Responses

When you ask your students a series of higher level thinking questions about a critical goal of a standard, they can answer with response cards. Give the students index cards that they label A, B, C, and D. They respond to your questions by holding up their answer card. For example, ask them, "The theme of the conflict between one's dreams and reality plays a major role in all of these except, A—*A Midsummer Nights' Dream;* B—*Of Mice and Men;* C—*Don Quixote;* and D—*Toning the Sweep.*" Count the correct answers for each question and calculate the percent of the class answering correctly. For example, if 15 out of 25 students answer the first question correctly (60%), 20 answer the second question (80%), and 5 answer the third question (20%), then their class average score for all three questions is 53%. You can set up a spreadsheet (shown in Figure 2.4) to quickly calculate the class percentage of students successfully answering the questions; you enter the questions going down the first column and the A, B, C, D choices going across. You can inform the class of its learning status.

Figure 2.4. Spreadsheet of Student Responses

English 3.3: Critical Analysis/Class Analysis Number of students selecting each choice. The correct answers are in **bold.**			
	A	B	C	D
Question 1	**15**	4	4	2
Question 2	1	**20**	4	0
Question 3	5	8	7	**5**

When you observe that all of your students are answering the higher-level thinking questions about a critical aspect of the standard, then you can assume that they have already made progress in the standard. You will need more in-depth observation before you feel confident that they have achieved the standard. Based on the scores for each question, you can determine some standard goal areas in which they will need some refocusing. If fewer than all students successfully answer these in-depth probing questions about the standard, then you will want to think of some additional strategies to help those students who have not been successful so far.

If your school has a personal response system or "clickers," then your students can respond electronically; you and your students instantly see the class results that serve as a starting point for their growth in that standard. The class responses for each choice will be shown instantly.

Rate Discussions

As you ask questions, make comments, or engage the students in a class verbal standards-based activity, you can do a quick check off of the students' academic response in terms of the standards-based question or statement. You can use a class list or a seating chart either in a physical paper form or in a digital form to record the code for each student who responds (Herman, Aschbacher, & Winters, 1992):

4—Complete response

3—Response that demonstrates an understanding or application of the goal

2—Minimal evidence (partial or over-general response)

1—No evidence

For example, Mrs. Martinez asks her elementary school math students to explore the various ways in which apples are packaged, the amount of apples in each package, and how this explains measurement. She has numerous apple packages such as a bushel, box, peck, large plastic bag, and small paper bag, all containing the same type of apple. As she listens to her students expressing their thoughts, she marks down on her class seating chart their responses using the 4, 3, 2, or 1 coding (Figure 2.5). This seating chart only shows the first two rows of students.

Figure 2.5. Rate Discussions Using a Seating Chart

Flores, Tina 4	Velez, Maria 3	Olsoma, Ben 2	Uter, Manco 3	Hanson, Mick 1
Evans, Dale 3	Lee, Kim 4	Jones, Lisa 1	Jordon, Nikki 3	Yacob, Roz 2

Agree-Disagree

You can use the agree-disagree format (Willis, 2006) to rate questions. After you ask a question to the whole class, wait for your students to think, and then call on a student who gives an answer. Next ask students to raise their hands if they agree with this answer. You might ask a follow-up question that focuses on possible misconceptions and repeat the process, or you may ask a more advanced question. By watching the students' hands, you have a beginning idea of overall class knowledge level. For example, as a high school music teacher who wants to see how well students are progressing in the National Standard for Music standard of "Listening to, analyzing and describing music," you ask "Tempo is to speed as dynamic is to ____?" Give thinking time, call on a student to respond, and then ask the class if they agree with his or her response. Then you can ask students to explain their thinking.

Sample

You can use the sample format (Hunter, 1982) for assessing questions. After you ask a question to the whole class, ask all the students to think and then call on a student who gives an answer. Next call on at least four or more students for their answers before you respond. If you notice a pattern in the students' answers, you may ask more students. By asking at least five students, you sample the class. If you ask 5 out of 30 students, you have asked approximately 17% of your class. If you ask a similar question or a more in-depth question and ask five more students, you quickly develop a feeling for how well the class (at least 34% of it) understands the standards-based concept. You offer instant formative suggestions to overcome the incorrect pattern that you noticed. For example, as an elementary teacher whose class works on the Ohio social studies standard of "Explain the reasons people from various cultural groups came to North America and the consequences of their interactions with each other" (Ohio State Department of Education, 2007), you show a list of five statements and ask a student to tell you how many of these are facts. Then ask five more students. You may go back and ask the students to explain their reasoning for their answers.

Think-Pair-Share

After giving the class a topic, have students form groups of two (a pair). They have several minutes to individually think about the topic, then they share or talk it over with their partner. They write out a quick report. Call on some students from various groups for their group report. For example, you ask your high school art students to compare and contrast the art of two Spanish artists, Picasso and Goya. Listen as they describe the similarities and differences in terms of visual, spatial, temporal, and functional areas as specified in the National Art Education Standard. Determine what specific assistance certain groups need based on their answers.

Think Aloud

The "think aloud" works like this; as a student (or students) reads, does, or thinks through a process, he or she orally says his or her thoughts (Alaska Department of Education & Early Development, 1996). Listen carefully, noting strengths in the students' thinking and identifying possible misconceptions or ineffective learning strategies.

Think alouds can take many different forms in your classroom. In a think–talk project, the students explain how they do a process or use a strategy. For example in your elementary science class, after you give Pablo 10 cards of different animals and 4 different habitat cards, you ask him to sort the animals according to the habitat and to explain what he thinks as he sorts. When you use a "project-interview think aloud," you delve into the student's higher level standards-based thinking about a project. Ask the student questions that start with "Why" and "How," or phrase questions that require higher-level thinking skills such as comparing and contrasting. As a social studies teacher, for example, you may ask your student about his immigration project with these two questions: "What do the different waves of immigrants have in common?" and "How are they different?"

Count

A partner serves as a counter for an activity to analyze the quality or quantity of the response. For example, an English as other language student, Georgios, asks as many questions about a picture as he can in a minute. His partner, Tereza, checks off each different question word on the list of question words as he says it. At the end of a minute, Tereza gives him the feedback such as "You used all the question words" or "You used all the question words except 'Why'?" As the counter reports back the number to you or on a checklist, you can determine which students need specific practice in becoming more fluent on certain conversation topics; then you can plan to group them together so you can offer them specific suggestions. You might ask the whole class to share their strategies for saying many sentences so that the nonfluent students can benefit from their specific suggestions; they can all become proficient in the standard of "present information, concepts, and ideas to an audience of listeners or readers on a variety of topics" (Standard 1.3) (Missouri Department of Elementary and Secondary Education, 2001).

Take a Three-Minute Pulse

After 10 to 15 minutes of a demonstration, lecture, or reading, stop the class and ask the students to reflect on and verbalize about something they learned in terms of higher-level thinking (Marzano & Pickering 1997). For example, after you have shown them a movie clip about the colonization of North America, ask them "What evidence is there of this type of colonization in today's culture?" Marzano (1997) suggests prompts such as these to help guide the learners:

How does this information relate to you?

How does what we've just learned relate to...?

How is what we've just learned similar or different to...?

Identify one thing you already knew and something that was new to you. (p. 400)

You can have the students write down their names and write out their answers so you can quickly look over their reflections before you determine the next phase of instruction.

Confer about Learning

Schedule time to meet with each student to review their standards-based progress. In these two- to five-minute meetings, you ask the students how well they think they are progressing and review the data from all their previous assessments as part of the monitoring process. Then help the student create a plan for improvement. For example, during your scheduled time with Madhavi to go over her progress in your music classroom, she displays what she has done according to the standards' checklist and explains to you her evidence, such as her recording of rhythm patterns played on the class instruments. Listen to her evidence to verify that she has achieved the goals in the checklist and ask her questions about her other evidence.

Ask Direct Questions

Use this student speaking assessment when you want to discern the level of a student's knowledge. For example, as an art teacher, you can ask a student to tell the differences between the classical and the baroque style of painting. As a Spanish teacher, you can ask a student to tell about a problem at the bank by using at least eight bank vocabulary words. Listen to see if the student can correctly use the words in a meaningful story about the bank to practice the standard that focuses on conversing about common topics.

Converse, Dialogue, or Role Play

Students can role play as you listen to their thinking. After a class discussion on the monetary system in your social studies economics class, ask your students to role play a situation in which some citizens are trying to convince a city common council to create its own money like the "Ithaca Hours" (a local currency in Ithaca, New York where 1 hour of work equals $10). Some students role play council members, others become local business people, others assume the role of bankers, and some role play citizens. Listen carefully to discern their understanding of the monetary system, and record a plus sign (+) for a proficient understanding of the monetary system) or a minus sign (–) for a nonproficient understanding next to each student's name each time he or she speaks. For any minus sign, note the learning gap.

Observe What Students Do

Every class provides you with valuable information on your students' academic progress through what they do in your classroom. As you walk around the room, observe the students' standard work. You will probably limit your observation to one standard and, more likely, to one goal of the standard.

A few things you can observe are listed in Figure 2.6.

Figure 2.6. Monitor What Students Do

_____	Total physical response	_____	Hand signals for music conducting
_____	Model building	_____	Movement to answer corners
_____	Simulations	_____	Role playing
_____	Demonstration	_____	Reenactment
_____	Game playing	_____	Lab or other set up
_____	Picture sorting	_____	Interviews
_____	Think-Pair-Share	_____	Measurement
_____	Gestures to show ideas	_____	Placement of sticky notes on a wall
_____	Matching answers to questions cards	_____	Steps in a sports move (layup shot)
_____	Other _____	_____	Other _____

Observations of students can take many different forms from little structure (open ended) to medium structure to highly structured (checklists).

Record Anecdotal Information

What standards-based student information can you describe briefly in objective and measurable terms based on what you observe (a student anecdote)? For example, you want to observe how well your high school science groups set up a lab on wave motion, so you observe who does what, how carefully, and in what order. You may observe how a particular student or a group of students in your social studies class works together on organizing their research cards (Greater Saskatoon Catholic Schools, n.d.).

Anecdotal observations vary from observations using very open-ended forms to very structured listings to observe for learning. The following form (Figure 2.7) provides you with an open-ended format so that you can write whatever you observe. For example, you watch an elementary math student, Asha, as she uses her manipulatives to show various ways that 20 can be formed with the math manipulatives.

Figure 2.7. Anecdotal Observation—Open-Ended Form

Student: _____ Date: _____

Observer: _____

Standard task: _____

_____

Class setting: _____

_____

What the student did in terms of the standard:

_____

_____

Notes/recommendations/actions:

_____

_____

A semi-structured anecdotal form (Figure 2.8) may include several specific categories for which to observe but uses only two specific areas to observe within each category. For example, as your class explores the social studies geography standard of "understands that culture and experience influence people's perceptions of places and regions" from the MCREL standards (2008), use part of the Library of Congress's Image of Our People Teacher Anecdotal Record (n.d.).

Figure 2.8. Teacher Anecdotal Record—Semi-Structured

Student: _____ Date:_____

Standard: Understands that culture and experience influence people's perceptions of
places and regions

Did student choose a photograph and share/discuss it within the group?

Positive results:

Problems:

Did student study the photograph and complete the photograph analysis?

Positive results:

Problems:

When you use a very structured anecdotal record such as Figure 2.9, you may be using a checklist, scale, "I can" listing, or rubric that has spaces for your comments on the student's work. You might create this checklist at Project Based Learning (n.d.) and then modify it into a structured analysis anecdotal record that you use as you observe your science students in their lab. Students can use this form to self-assess their safety. Note that the following is a partial listing.

Figure 2.9. Anecdotal Record—Very Structured

"I can"	Name:_____	Date:_____
Yes/No	Elementary Science Safety Checklist	Comments
	I wore goggles.	
	I carried things with two hands.	
	I told my teacher about any accidents.	
	I did not hide any accident or spills.	
	I walked and did not run.	

Observe Physical Responses

You can select from many physical response strategies for students:

♦ Students use their bodies to respond to your question or statement, and you can quickly scan the class to see who understands the concept. For example, in your middle school science class, as you say "olfactory," students point to their noses. Your math students demonstrate acute, obtuse, and right angles with their arm by using their elbow to change the angle; they use both arms to demonstrate their knowledge of squares and rectangles. Likewise, a group of students can use their bodies, without moving or talking, to convey the standard concept in a human tableau or frieze. As each group forms a frieze to depict a scene from a story in English class such a scene from *Macbeth*, other class members identify who each student represents in the scene, what happens in the scene, and what emotion each character displays. You can scan to see the level of their understanding.

♦ Small groups demonstrate all the steps in a process or procedure through role playing or demonstration. Students act out the steps in a certain chemical reaction or the process that a bill goes through to become a law. Observe each group's demonstration to identify their present status in regard to the standard and what gaps they need to close to reach the standard.

♦ Students can build a model (Meier in Erwin, 2004). After you describe a concept, process, or skill, your students build a model using paper, paper clips, clay, paper plates, cups, wooden sticks, or any other material. Then they explain their model to the class. For example, elementary science students build a model to show gravity. Middle school social students can create a model of an energy-efficient future city.

What Students Produce (Their Work)

Observe students' learning through what they produce in class. When you have students do projects at Bloom's higher levels of thinking (1956), you have a greater insight into their standards-based thinking. Perhaps you engage your students in authentic tasks that duplicate real life experiences in the classroom. For example, your math students analyze the local traffic flow in front of the school and figure out alternative traffic patterns. You can observe their thinking in this complex task that involves numerous related skills.

As with any differentiated class, when students have choices they can explore the learning standard in their own preferred way of learning. Whether students do a poster, a Power Point presentation, a webcast, podcast, or drawing, they still demonstrate the same standard learning, and you can observe their work for where they are in the standard.

You can assess students' learning through looking at student's work. Some examples are shown in Figure 2.10.

Figure 2.10. Monitor What Students Produce

_____	Homework	_____	Project
_____	Essay	_____	Poem
_____	Concept map	_____	Drawing of a concept
_____	Summary of an event	_____	Power Point presentation
_____	Portfolio	_____	Letter
_____	Journal	_____	Note
_____	Poster	_____	Color coding of important items
_____	Blog or wiki entry	_____	E-movie or YouTube video
_____	Annotation of their bookmarks	_____	Videoconference preparation
_____	Other _____	_____	Other _____

Become Inquiring Minds

For the inquiring minds activity (Erwin, 2004), students work in a small group. Each student has the role of either reader, inquirer, answerer, or friend. The reader reads aloud a passage from the class assignment. The inquirer writes a question about the passage on an index card. The answerer reads aloud the question, answers the question or uses a friend or the group to help him or her answer it. If the group agrees that the answer is correct, the answerer writes it down. You can provide the students with question starters such as when, where, why, and how, and "How is this different from...?" Furthermore, you can assign a point value to each type of question they ask so that as the students ask and answer higher level thinking questions, they receive more points. Students can be instructed to reach a number such as 200 points. Erwin (2004) proposes the following scoring:

Knowledge—5 points   Comprehension—10 points

Application—15 points   Analysis—20 points

Synthesis—25 points   Evaluation—30 points (pp. 86–87)

By looking at what questions they asked and how well they answered those questions, you can quickly gage the academic progress of a group and be prepared to give them specific formative feedback. For example, after elementary students have read their social studies book chapter about China, they do the inquiring minds activity to reveal their thinking about China.

Draw for Understandings

You can examine what the students know or can do about a standard goal by having them illustrate an idea, concept, or process with few or no words. Elementary science students can draw the orbit of the earth around the sun, and hold it up, so you can glance at all of their drawings at once. They can compare their drawings to the drawings of others to see if their illustration is comprehensive and also detailed enough. You can explain to the whole class any misconceptions you see or explain any missing logic from their drawings. In a variation, after 10 minutes of your presentation, stop and ask the students to draw what they have understood.

Provide Group Instructional Feedback

A group leader helps the group to analyze what they know or can do, what problems there are, and how these learning problems can be fixed (Yee, n.d.). Often various group members have solutions to each other's learning problems. The group leader prepares a report to you using your standard performance indicators form. For example, to determine how much your high school English class has progressed toward Standard 2: Personal Expression, you have the group and group leader check off the skills that all group members can presently demonstrate.

In the following partial list for poetry, a check mark (✓) means all group members can do the learning task and a blank line means all students have not demonstrated this thus far.

- ✓ Identify the subject

- ✓ Identify the point of view

- ✓ Identify metaphors and similes

- __ Identify the central metaphor of the poem

- __ Explain how the images in the poem support the central metaphor

- __ Identify the tone

Based on this report, you can focus your feedback for the improvement of this group.

Peer Evaluate

Give your students a checklist or rubric and ask them to evaluate the work of another student. Your checklist or rubric has to be able to be clearly understood and contain objective statements that can be easily observed and measured. A science student may do a checklist of another student's lab report on water erosion with a simple "present" or "not present." If there is a "not present," the student explains what needs to be included for the lab report to be at the proficient level.

Figure 2.11 shows a partial lab report checklist.

Figure 2.11. Peer Lab Report Checklist

Indicate with a "P" (present) or "N" (not present). For any "N," tell what is missing.

___ Name of lab	If N, missing _____
___ Purpose of lab	If N, missing _____
___ Hypothesis	If N, missing _____
___ Background/theory	If N, missing _____
___Procedures/methods	If N, missing _____

Journal

Students are asked to do a quick "journal write" during the class or at the end of class about the learning tasks. Jensen in Erwin (2004) suggests these journaling prompts connect to previous learning; connect to content from another subject area; assess what they will do or feel in that situation; tie it to personal values; and relate it in three ways to their own lives. For example, as a high school music teacher, you play the song, "You've Got to Be Carefully Taught" from *South Pacific* and ask the students to connect it to another event from history. Read their journals as they listen to another song from the musical and then decide how to help the class to improve in "understanding music in relation to history and culture" standard from the National Standards for Music Education.

Write Diagnostic Learning Logs

Students can keep diagnostic learning logs (Figure 2.12). For example, as science students listen to a lecture or presentation on the function of a cell, they write down the major concepts in one list on the left side and then they write down in the center what they are unsure of or what questions they have. They reflect on and analyze the major concepts to determine if they can answer their own uncertainties. They try to diagnose their learning weaknesses and record these in the third column as shown in the following chart. Students learn to help self-correct themselves for each standard.

Figure 2.12. Diagnostic Learning Log

Major Concepts	Unsure or Questions	My Solutions

Calkins' double-entry ledger model (1986) in which English language arts students have three columns presents a variation on the diagnostic learning logs. As illustrated in Figure 2.13, the first column presents the text, the next has the students' immediate reaction, and the third contains the students' reaction after reflection:

Figure 2.13. Double-Entry Ledger Model

Text	Immediate Reaction	Reaction after Reflection

Concept Map

Students display their thinking in visual form when they use concept maps (a technique for visualizing the relationship among concepts). According to Parrott (n.d.), students can select from a multitude of maps such as brainstorming (concept map and mind maps), sequence (time line, cycle, flow chart, hierarchical, and chain), compare and contrast (Venn circles, Venn boxes, attributes, and T-charts), and analysis (PMI—Plus, Minus, Interesting, and KWL—Know, Want to know, and Learned). For example, when a student, Martina, compares the various features of a particular concept such as which animals have the follow traits of a mammal, she uses an attribute concept map known as a "semantic features analysis," which is shown in Figure 2.14. She checks off the feature that each animal has.

Figure 2.14. Semantic Features Analysis

	Produces Milk	Has Hair/Fur	Has Teeth	Is Warm-Blooded
Dog				
Frog				
Elephant				
Bird				

You quickly look at her chart to see what she has learned regarding this part of the standard.

Check Homework

You can check each student's homework quickly to see the successes and the areas for improvement. You may check on only the last two questions, questions which build on all the information in the learning material, or questions that may be the "trickiest" for the students. As an elementary math teacher you may only look at the last odd problem and the last even problem, which include several math functions in the same problem. You can use your class list to keep track of students who are not proficient in these skills so that you can group these students for specific assistance.

Turn in an Exit Sheet

Before the students can exit out the door, they summarize the major concepts, list the major steps in a process, contrast what they have learned today to another concept, or explain a complex task in writing. They do this in one to two minutes. When you ask questions at the thinking level of application, analysis, synthesis, or evaluation, you have more insight into their deep thinking about the topic. You may ask your high school art students, "How does cubism show up in Diego Rivera's mural work?" Before their next class, read over the papers and divide the students into a group who understood the concept and a group who did not. Another form of the exit sheet can be a one-minute essay in which students write at any time during the class on a topic that involves higher-level thinking such as when you ask them to compare famous sidekicks such as Sancho Panza from *Don Quixote* and George from *Of Mice and Men*.

Reflect Through One-Minute Confusion Paper

Students respond in writing in one minute to the three questions that you post such as, "What I learned today?," "What I am unclear/unsure about?," and "Comments." For example, after you have demonstrated acids in your science class, you ask students to do a one-minute paper. As the students do another quick task in the classroom such as reading a few pages about chemical reactions from their textbook, rapidly look at their papers to see if they are progressing in the day's tasks, what areas they indicate as needing clarification, and other issues that they include. You can redirect your teaching to address major problems before you continue the Physical Science Content Standard B: Chemical Reactions (National Committee on Science Education Standards and Assessment, National Research Council, 1998).

Build In Portfolio Planning Days

To structure the portfolio process (materials that demonstrate in an organized manner the achievement of a certain standard or standards) for either paper or electronic portfolios for your students, you can build in portfolio planning days (Tuttle, 2007b). For example, you may have one portfolio planning day each quarter for your year-long course. You supply the students with a physical or virtual form to help them think through the process as show in Figure 2.15. You observe their form to assess their learning.

Figure 2.15. Portfolio Planning Form

Standard: _____

Possible evidence (assignments or in class work) that I have collected for this standard:

_____   _____

_____   _____

I have chosen the evidence of _____ for the

portfolio. This evidence demonstrates the standard because:

_____

I may need more evidence for this standard since my present evidence

_____

After students have put their first round of evidence in their e-portfolios, the next e-portfolio review days reveal their ability to discriminate between the quality of their more recent work and the past work that they already have in the portfolio.

Review a Learning Contract

When students review their learning contract (a working agreement between a student and teacher focusing on how that student will meet specific learning objectives) with you, you have an opportunity to hear their learning. For example, your student, Jung, explains to you what he has already accomplished and what he has yet to accomplish as part of his standards-based learning contract for the changing theories of evolution science unit. Because you have written the learning contract by listing performance tasks that you have taken from your seventh grade Georgia Science Standards, you quickly determine Jung's progress in the standard (Georgia Department of Education, 2006).

> S7L5. Students will examine the evolution of living organisms through inherited characteristics that promote survival of organisms and the survival of successive generations of their offspring.
>
> a. Explain that physical characteristics of organisms have changed over successive generations (e.g., Darwin's finches and peppered moths of Manchester).
>
> b. Describe ways in which species on earth have evolved due to natural selection.
>
> c. Trace evidence that the fossil record found in sedimentary rock provides evidence for the long history of changing life forms.

How Students Answer Test Questions

A test reveals much about the students' standard-based learning when a test focuses on thinking skills instead of just factual information. For example, you do not test your students on all the major battles in the U.S. Civil War because the results do not help you to identify if the students can understand the causes of conflicts, which is the learning goal. You do test them on the differences between the causes of the U.S. Civil War and of the War of 1812 to focus on the conflicts.

If you structure your test from easy (lower-level thinking) to hard (higher-level thinking), you can begin to see where your students are on the learning continuum for the standard. For example, in a French class, the first three questions are on verb meanings such as "travailler = to work;" the next three are on verb forms such as the verb in the "I" form; and the last three questions require the student to use the verb in sentences about a job. You can analyze your questions by recording them on the following Bloom's (1956) chart (Figure 2.16). You list the category of questions in the first column and you indicate how many questions fall into each of the three Bloom's levels that go across. By scanning where the correct answers are, you can discern the students' level of learning.

Figure 2.16. Analyzing Test Questions Using Bloom

Question	Knowledge/ Comprehension	Application/ Analysis	Synthesis/ Evaluation
Verb meaning	3		
Verb forms		3	
Verbs in sentences			3

You can add the dimension of the students' confidence in their answers to your test to find out even more about the process. You may have a scale of 4 (I am confident about the answer), 3 (I am fairly certain about my answer), 2 (I'm making a guess), and 1 (I have no idea).

Your test question and a confidence rating for your fifth grade math class looks like:

____ Manchester has 69,108 people and Shortsville has 42,759 people. How much bigger is Manchester than Shortsville? (A) 27,459 (B) 10,8457 (C) 111,867 (D) 26,349

____ Confidence rating (4, 3, 2, 1)

Ask Topic Questions

To determine the depth of student understanding about the topic, ask the student to write five probing questions about the topic (Angelo & Cross, 1993). The students are not to ask factual questions such as "Who did something?" or "When it was done?," but they are to write questions such as "Why did the Catholics Kings agree to fund Columbus' trip?" Your review of the individual student's probing questions can reveal how in-depth each student is thinking about the critical aspects of this global analysis of world history standard.

Use a Formative Assessment Test Bank

Your state education department, such as the Arizona Department of Education (2007), may have its own bank or collection of standards-based questions from which you can select your test questions for a particular standard. Likewise, your school district may subscribe to a service such as Pearson (2007) that allows you to select from its standards question bank. Customize your tests, and the students take the tests online or in paper format. When the students do the assessment online, the system analyzes the results for you.

Small Group, Peer, and Self-Monitoring

Students can learn to monitor each other and themselves through a series of standards-based learning experiences.

Test in a Collaborative Group

In testing in a collaborative group (Meier in Erwin, 2004), prepare a short test that has a multiple-choice or short-answer format. To access the students' prior learning, they work on this individually in pencil and then work on it collaboratively in their group with a pen. After a few minutes, go over the test with the class with each student answering a question. For example, your science test on the solar system may include questions such as:

Our solar system contains the sun, the _____, and _____

An example of a repeating pattern in our solar system that is visible from earth is

_____.

"Night" happens when _____

_____

"Summer" happens when _____

_____ _____

A star is different from a planet because _____

_____ _____

Collect the test to better assess each student's present learning status.

Write a Test in Pairs

Ask students to write test questions for the unit based on your structure (Willis, 2006, p. 91). Your instructions specify the type of questions they will ask such as, "include 15 calculations and 5 word problems from 2 of each of the 5 subsections of the chapter." Collect their papers and change their numbers. Return the papers to the students, who, for homework rewrite their tests with the new numbers. In class, they form pairs, exchange their practice tests, peer correct, and help their partners to learn how to do the problem correctly. Likewise, you can specify the type of thinking that you want to see in their test questions such as, include three compare and contrast questions out of the five questions. By looking at their questions, you can identify the progress of the students in the standard.

Self-Checks During Class

Students can do various self-checks during class:

- After students show you they have done their homework, they compare their progress against a physical or digital notebook that has some self-check questions and some answers. For example, Natasha checks her high school global history religions contrast chart against the class example and finds out that she has not included a critical category so she adds it to become proficient (Willis, 2006, p. 84).

- After you show students the answer or solution, they can ask for clarification with a word such as "verification," when they want to see how a problem was done. Likewise, they can color code their work. The math students highlight in yellow for a careless error such as switching numbers and in red for an incomplete comprehension error such as not understanding the process. Scan their papers to see where the colors are to plan how you can better help your students learn (Clarke, 2005).

- Students self-assess their present learning status when you give them a checklist with clearly defined items, and they indicate if they have or have not done the items such as having a topic sentence. Verify their checklist.

- They self-assess themselves on an assessment tool at the midpoint of the project, indicate what they need to do to improve to be proficient in the standard and create a work plan for those improvements. Look over each student's self-assessment and make sure that their planned activities will result in their being successful in the standard.

Self-Assess the Learning

Students answer questions about their learning to give you greater insights into their learning (Cummings, 2000):

+ What did I learn today?

+ What do I feel that I can do now?

+ What am I not sure of or confused about? Can I figure it out by myself or do I need outside help?

+ What do I need assistance with? What type assistance do I need: Internet, textbook, study guide, concept map, a peer or the teacher?

+ What am I going to do to improve in this standard? When will I start? What do I need? (p. 28)

Recording the Observations

For you to establish patterns of growth and to identify learning gap patterns, you need to have enough data. If you collect even one piece of data on a student a day, by the end of the week you will have five pieces of data. No student will fall between the cracks if you constantly monitor each student. However, all these formative assessments will not benefit you if you do not record the vast amount of data that you collect on each student.

If you are assessing the same key goal of the standard, you can have a checklist in which you record a one (1) for being proficient and a zero (0) for not being proficient or a proficiency scale of 1 to 4 with 4 for above-proficient work that you record each day. You can use a list of performance indicators for each goal to monitor the students' progress from low-level thinking tasks up to higher level thinking ones.

Record Using Low- to High-Technology Approaches

Your approach to recording your standards-based observations can be low-tech or high-tech. You may use 3 by 5 cards or sticky notes as you walk around the classroom. After writing down the student's initials and the date, you write down the brief observation, for example, Jane's preciseness in measuring, Carlos' explanation of a problem to another student, or Mia's accurate drawing of a simple machine. After class, during your planning period, or at the end of the day, you put each student's sticky note in his or her alphabetically arranged page in your class-assessment binder. One variation on the sticky notes involves printing the week's date, the performance tasks for the week, and some lines for your observations on index cards or slips of paper. Attach those cards or slips to the student's sheet in the binder. Another strategy involves writing your observation notes on a computer mail label and then putting the label on the student's page in the binder.

You may prefer to enter the notes directly on the student's page in the binder that you carry. You might assess a student against a checklist and then add that checklist to the student's section in a binder. By word processing these observations that you put on sticky notes, index cards, or mail labels, you can organize and sort the students' observations to see patterns over time.

Figure 2.17 is an example of index card monitoring where you write your many observations on the one standard for a specific student.

Figure 2.17. Index Card Monitoring

Name: _____	Standard goal: _____
1	2
3	4
5	6
7	8
9	10

On the high-tech side, when you enter the observation information directly from your PDA, tablet or classroom computer into a word processor, database, spreadsheet, or assessment system, then you do not waste time in recopying information. In addition, you can do instant sorts to find out if the student has displayed similar performance problems or achievements in the past. Make it a practice to review each student's formative assessments on a regular basis so that you can provide a better learning experience for the student. If you have recorded in your word processor, database, or spreadsheet, the strategy you and the student agreed on the last time to help the student improve in the standard, and you do not see any improvement, suggest another learning strategy.

For example, in your science middle school classroom your students are designing a machine. Observe and write down a comment every other day so that within a two-week period, you have many observations as shown in Figure 2.18.

Figure 2.18. Science Observations Over Time

Observations for Bernard from Period 2

Name	Date	Unit	Observation
W, B.	11/12/07	Forces	Asked 2 why questions of team
W, B.	11/14/07	Forces	Did math wrong twice
W, B.	11/16/07	Forces	Drew his own force machine
W, B.	11/19/07	Forces	Machine didn't work, math off
W, B.	11/21/07	Forces	Figured out why peer's machine didn't work
W, B.	11/23/07	Forces	His partially worked

Based on your observations in your second period science class, you can more easily detect the pattern that Bernard deals well with high-level thinking, but he needs improvement in the math goal of his science. Once you find a topic such as math in the observation, search for other math references and then analyze the pattern.

Use a Checklist

Additionally, you can use a checklist to observe for certain standards-based skills such as oral communication over time (Tuttle, 2004). Your checklist can be as simple as a "O" for observed or "N" for not observed or as complex as a scale of Always, Most of the time, Sometimes, or Never for each performance task. If you use a numeric scale and record this on a computer, then the computer can do averages for you for each area of this communication standard. Figure 2.19 is a partial checklist for 10 oral communication observations.

Likewise, students can peer and self-monitor and record that information.

Figure 2.19. Oral Communication Over Time Checklist

Name: _____   Period: _____

Coding: 4 = Always, 3 = Most of the time, 2 = Sometimes/rarely, 1 = Never

	Date	Date	Date	Date	Date	Date	Date	Date	Date
Communicating through speaking English Language Arts 1.1									
Contributes a new idea or perspective									
Gives reasons or examples to support the idea									
Asks for clarification when needed									
Disagrees politely with another person by providing alternative examples or reasoning									

Record Students' Standard Observations Over Time

A starting point for doing, recording, and analyzing formative assessment in your classroom is the "every two weeks" method (Tuttle, 2007d). Within each two-week period do a formative assessment on the same critical standard and record that information in a grade book, spreadsheet, or database. Record a rating and a quick comment for each student. Repeat this each two-week cycle for three more cycles each time integrating the assessment in the content of the unit. For example, assess the students on the English Standard of Information and Understanding and, in particular, the students' ability to listen and then to agree or disagree with the information in a written paragraph as this also shows up on the state assessment. After you analyze the students' ratings, determine what one area would help the most students to improve in this standards activity, and do some activities to help the students master those goals necessary for success in this standard. You have identified certain students who will receive your small group or one-on-one help within the next two weeks. Repeat this similar standards-based assessment activity three more times during the next six weeks (one time each two weeks). By the end of eight weeks, you will have four formative assessments on a particular standard. For those students who have grown in the standard, celebrate their growth, and for those students who have not yet shown proficiency in the standard, plan a structured approach for their improvement. This every-two-weeks assessment model can work in all subjects that have essential standards such as physical safety in physical education, the inquiry process in science, essay writing in English, and analysis of primary documents in social studies. Constant monitoring leads to student success.

Summary

To establish where your students are in their learning progression, you and your students can observe students' learning through what they say, do, produce, or answer on tests. There are many different ways to monitor.

- ◆ In-depth learning experiences reveal more of students' thinking and therefore, provide better opportunities for observations.

- ◆ These observations take place during the class as students are doing learning activities.

- ◆ There are many ways to record your observation from paper-and-pencil to easy-to-use technology so that you can observe patterns over time in your students' learning.

3

Formative Assessment: Diagnosis

Overview
- ◆ Setting the Stage
- ◆ Questions
- ◆ Introduction
- ◆ Diagnostic Analysis
- ◆ Diagnostic Moving Forward
- ◆ Summary

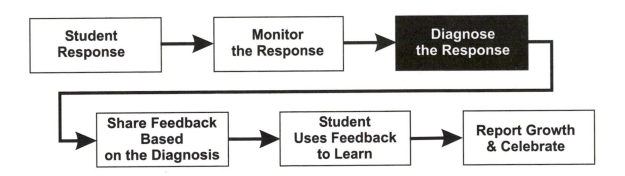

Setting the Stage

Mr. Watson and Mrs. Holmes look over their students' essays. Mr. Watson circles all the errors and returns the papers. Mrs. Holmes circles the major writing problems and labels each specific learning gap such as "lacks a topic sentence" or "run-on sentence." This diagnosis prepares her to select the formative feedback to help her students overcome their learning gaps.

Questions

♦ How do you and your students diagnose students' work?

♦ What tools can help in the diagnosis?

Introduction

Once you have observed students' learning, move on to diagnosing (interpreting, examining, figuring out the gaps in) the students' learning. When you diagnose, identify the present status of the students in terms of the standard. See what strengths the students presently possess and what areas are not yet developed. Understand where the students are in the learning journey. In addition, decide what strategies will help the students to move forward in their learning.

The difference between observing and diagnosing is the same as the difference between a nurse taking your vital signs and the doctor reacting to your vitals; someone watching you swing a golf club and that person being able to figure out how to help you improve your swing; or a photographer who looks at one of her pictures and then decides what to do better the next time. The more carefully you have observed the students' learning over time, the better you can accurately diagnose the students' status and help the students move forward in their learning.

Examine the Role of Diagnosis in Formative Assessment

Effective formative assessment not only provides "early warning" features that allow problems to be diagnosed promptly so that you, your students, and their parents know what extra effort the students need, but it also moves you and your students from thinking about the data to acting on the data by implementing a plan (Johnson, 2005). When you have ongoing formative assessment in the class, you identify the point at which learning falters, analyze how to help the students, and provide instant feedback to help the students to walk or even run with their learning (New Zealand Council for Educational Research, 2001). In your differentiated classroom, you continuously examine ongoing assessment data for students as a mean of adapting "up-front" teaching plans so that your plans address particular learning needs now and not at the end of the unit, semester, or year. (Tomlinson & McTighe, 2006).

Diagnostic Analysis

Diagnosis consists of you or your students interpreting the students' work and then you or your students determining how to help the students to move forward in their learning journey. In the first diagnosis part, you employ many strategies and your expertise.

Use Your Expertise

Your academic and pedagogical expertise makes formative assessment work. The more you know about your standards-based content area, the better you can diagnose students' work. A teacher who knows little about photography will not be able to do a thorough diagnosis of students' work in a high school art photography course. This art teacher may want to widen her knowledge base by comparing the information from the textbook with information from other sources. In a similar manner, she can develop a more comprehensive view of various strategies for teaching the standard by looking at how other teachers have approached the same lesson through visiting online websites. Also, your academic and pedagogical skills in drawing inferences from students' responses are crucial to the effectiveness of formative assessment. When you infer what the right gap is between the current and desired goal, you prepare yourself to give meaningful feedback that will move the students forward in their learning (Heritage, 2007b).

Consider General Formative Learning Issues

Your students may not be proficient in their learning for several pedagogical reasons (Stiggins, 2007). They may not have a clear vision of the standard; your solution is to help them to reword the standards in their own words to make sure that they understand it. Likewise, they may not be clear about the quality expected of them; you walk them through an exemplar. Sometimes students have an incorrect view of the quality; you show them they need multiple examples to provide their point instead of just one example. Also, your students may have not been focused on the learning task; you ask them the purpose of the learning task. Additionally, students perform in a nonproficient manner on a task when they have not had enough practice or tasks to develop their learning; you provide a series of different tasks that scaffold the student to success.

Students' faulty thinking may explain the reason that your students are not performing standards-based learning well. Marzano (2007) suggests that students be taught to identify these areas in their own and other students' work: faulty logic such as contradictions; attacks such as arguing against the person and not the point; weak references such as bias; and misinformation such as confusing facts. Once the students can identify these reasons, then they can begin to improve their own learning.

Keep the Standards in Front of You

Without a clear focus on the standard, you cannot diagnose the students' learning. When you keep the standard mentally in front of you as you observe student work, you and the students can better diagnose the students' learning gap and diagnose those who benefit from enrichment. As you observe the students, you can ask yourself how this work shows the standard and what additional learning might be needed. You constantly use teacher and student standards-based talk because such talk helps keep them on their formative learning path. Your statements help them to know their "true north" for their learning (Covey, 1990).

Identify Missing Critical Goals

Sometimes your students get so caught up in the daily learning that they miss the bigger picture, and their work shows that they have missed a critical aspect. As an Ohio eighth-grade social studies teacher, identify the possible learning evidences for the general standard of history once you have seen the Ohio State Department of Education standard listing (2007). You have a checklist of all the required goals within the major standard so you can be confident that students have worked through all of the goals as indicated in the following:

Standard: History The First Global Age

2. Describe the political, religious and economic aspects of North American colonization including:

_____   a. Reasons for colonization, including religion, desire for land and economic opportunity;

_____   b. Key differences among the Spanish, French and British colonies;

_____   c. Interactions between American Indians and European settlers, including the agricultural and cultural exchanges, alliances and conflicts;

_____   d. Indentured servitude and the introduction and institutionalization of slavery;

_____   e. Early representative governments and democratic practices that emerged, including town meetings and colonial assemblies;

_____   f. Conflicts among colonial powers for control of North America.

Scaffold the Learning Experiences

As you plan your standards-based learning unit, develop scaffolds (temporary learning support as students develop new skills) to help students move forward in their learning so they do not get stuck academically. Scaffolds do not imply a step-by-step locked-in approach but more of a springboard approach. Lipton and Wellman (1998) offer these suggestions:

- Predict potential problem areas (In this standard, where might my students get stuck? What alternative paths can I give them to avoid getting stuck?)

- Analyze the task/process/content (How might I break this task/process/content into increments that the students can successfully do?)

- Identify strategies necessary for success (How do effective learners achieve success with this task/process? How will I share these strategies with my students?)

- Identify prerequisite learnings (What fundamental concepts, facts, knowledge, skills, attitudes are prerequisites to this learning?)

- Design prototypes (What models of process or products would support success?)

- Determine learner's focus (Where and how does the learner's attention need to be focused along the way?) (p. 14)

Determine Prerequisite Skills

In addition to the standards, have a list of the prerequisite skills required for the present learning standard. As you observe students, listen to them, see their work, or test them, check off any skills that are lacking or incomplete. Decide how you can help the students develop these skills. For example, you notice that in your elementary math class, Charlotte has trouble in measuring, and you want to identify what particular measuring skill she lacks. You use the School Improvement in Maryland website (2007) for assistance in identifying the prerequisite skills and create the following checklist.

Topic B. Measurement Tools Indicator 1. Measure in nonstandard units

Objective a. Measure length of objects and pictures of objects

Prerequisite Skills

Before students can successfully measure objects, they need to be able to

_____ compare objects by length   _____ sort objects by length

_____ order objects by length   _____ use mathematics vocabulary such as longer, shorter

They should be able to:

_____ Compare 2 objects (the pen is longer than the pencil) and them move on to 3 or 4 objects.

_____ Sort objects into 2 groups (as long as; not as long as); then into 3 groups

_____ Order objects by length

As you more carefully observe Charlotte, you realize that she does not compare objects. You ask her to put one end of each of her two different-sized pencils against a book and to move her finger to show the end of the each pencil. As she moves her finger, she sees the difference.

Identify Misconceptions

Another tool to help you diagnose the student's present state involves a listing of common misconceptions, misunderstandings, or errors that past students have demonstrated when working on this standard. These misconceptions might block your students from closing the learning gap.

The Committee on Undergraduate Science Education (1997) has identified different types of misconceptions that you can use as a starting point:

- ◆ Preconceived notions or popular conceptions rooted in everyday experiences. Example: Water flowing underground must flow in streams.

- ◆ Nonscientific beliefs or views learned by students from sources other than scientific education, such as religious or mythical teachings. Example: Offer an abbreviated history of the earth and life forms.

- ◆ Conceptual misunderstandings or not confronting paradoxes and conflicts resulting from their own preconceived notions and nonscientific beliefs. Example: Light is only reflected from shiny surfaces.

- ◆ Vernacular misconceptions or the use of words that mean one thing in everyday life and another in a scientific context (e.g., "work"). Example: Correct use of the term "glacier retreat."

- ◆ Factual misconceptions or untrue statements learned at an early age and not challenged until adulthood. Example: Lightning never strikes twice in the same place.

When you show students through mini-experiments that their misconception is inaccurate, then they can replace it with a correct conception. Many students believe that different-sized objects fall at different rates. You may have your science students find or make an iMovie of two different-sized objects falling and then have them look frame by frame as the objects hit the ground.

Triangulate

Triangulation of data (using multiple data sources) provides another strategy for diagnosis. To see if common trends emerge you can compare the results of listening to a student, looking at the student's work, watching the student doing something, and seeing the student's test results. For example, as you listen to your high school English students analyze a poem in a small group, as you look at their Venn diagram comparison for two poems, as you watch them match pictures to the poem's meaning or emotion, and as they take quizzes on poetry devices in poems, you have multiple types of evidence that all triangulate on their ability to analyze literature. You may find that all of these assessments show the same strengths and learning gaps; you may find that a particular assessment better pinpoints specific literary analysis problems. With a stronger formative diagnosis, you are better able to select an appropriate learning strategy to help the students' improve.

Observe Learning Over Time

When you or the students use the same assessment tool to observe the students' work over time, you verify that the students have already become proficient or that they are still developing. A one-time observation may not represent a students' learning pattern but a one-time only occurrence. For example, Johnnie may have received a below-proficient rating on his social studies transportation systems and population project because he was sick. When you and your students observe over time, you have a more complete picture of the students' learning. In addition, you and your students can see what changes have taken place by looking at the individual categories of the assessment tool. The long-range view enables you and the students to see if standards-based progress has been made.

By using a spreadsheet, you can keep your own classroom formative assessment information. Assessment data reveals a clearer picture when you have more than just one isolated piece of assessment data. Therefore, a truer picture of each student forms when you have entered the assessment data for several assessments into your computer spreadsheet as shown in Figure 3.1. The student names are in the column A, the first assessment for Standard 1.1 in column B, the second assessment in column C, and the next in column D, and so on. The task name is abbreviated, for example, "1.1ListWrit920" means "Standard 1.1 Students listen and then write, and they did it on Sept. 20," whereas "1.1LWRadi0923 means Standard 1.1. Listen and write using the radio on Sept. 23."

Figure 3.1. Listening Assessments Over Time Spreadsheet

	A	B	C	D
1				
2		1.1LisWrit920	1.1LWRad923	1.1LWTV927
3	Adams, Joe	90	90	100
4	Brown, Mary	70	80	85
5	Cooper, Frank	40	40	60
6	Donner, Flo	80	75	90
7	Edmond, Jose	85	90	95
8	Frank, Huan	60	70	80

To determine if the class progresses, all the columns can be averaged. Find the average for the column B by highlighting the numbers, go to Edit, select Function, and select Average. To copy this average to the other number columns, start by highlighting the average function in column B and continue to highlight all the columns to the right in which there are scores. Next go up to the top "Edit Menu" and select "Fill." Select the choice of "Right." The average function will be applied to all the columns in one easy click as illustrated in Figure 3.2.

Figure 3.2. Class Average Over Time Spreadsheet

	A	B	C	D
1				
2		1.1LisWrit920	1.1LWRad923	1.1LWTV927
3	Adams, Joe	90	90	100
4	Brown, Mary	70	80	85
5	Cooper, Frank	40	40	60
6	Donner, Flo	80	75	90
7	Edmond, Jose	85	90	95
8	Frank, Huan	60	70	80
9				
10	Average	70.83	74.17	85

As you look at the three assessment scores, you can see the class progress. The class average of 85 represents the goal. However, take a look at each individual to make sure that all the individuals have succeeded.

This time highlight all the students and their scores making sure not to include the labels at the top or the averages at the bottom. Go up to the top Data Menu and select Sort. This time sort from the most recent assessment backward to the first so you change the top sort to be column D, the next sort to be column C, and the last sort to column B. Confirm that you have checked the Ascending button. After you click on "OK," you see, as illustrated in Figure 3.3, the results with the students' lowest scores on top.

Figure 3.3. Student Scores Low to High Spreadsheet

	A	B	C	D
1				
2		1.1LisWrit920	1.1LWRad923	1.1LWTV927
3	Cooper, Frank	40	40	60
4	Frank, Huan	60	70	80
5	Brown, Mary	70	80	85
6	Donner, Flo	80	75	90
7	Edmond, Jose	85	90	95
8	Adams, Joe	90	90	100
9				
10	Average	70.83	74.17	85

Based on this new cumulative data for each student, you can rethink the next instructional strategy to help all students achieve the component goal. You can feel proud of the progress that the class, and more importantly, the individual students are making. With this data, you are keenly aware of which students will benefit from additional scaffolding and which students have already achieved success in this standard goal.

Diagnostic Moving Forward

After you and your students have observed and analyzed the students' learning, you and they identify what will help them to move forward in their learning. The following formative assessments help you all to go from just analysis to identifying what particular assistance the students need in their learning journey.

Use Quizzes

When students take a practice formative-based quiz or test, they and you can discover their strengths and learning gaps. Your quiz may go from the easy questions (knowledge and comprehension, such as math terms) to slightly more difficult (application and analysis, such as using a formula) to more complex (synthesis and evaluation, such as deciding which alternative to select). As you all look at which questions they answered correctly and incorrectly, you can pinpoint the cognitive level that they are at in terms of the goal and begin to identify specific strategies to help them increase in their level of thinking. Also, when you group similar concepts together, for example on a social studies test on South America, such as the first five questions on the geography and the next five on the economics, you can use the results of the quiz to help you determine their present status and if the concept has to be retaught using a different approach (Stronge, 2002).

When students take these quizzes online such as in Blackboard, they, and you, receive the results instantly so that you can begin a dialogue about improvement strategies. Furthermore, you can plan how to regroup students so that all students can show success in the standard through small group instruction. You may have already found or created multimedia tutorials on YouTube or other computer sites to provide essential scaffolding of learning.

Select New Success Strategy

After students do an assignment, they self-correct, reflect on why they did not perform proficiently, and select from some possible new strategies for their improvement. For example, as a middle school math teacher, you can provide students with these possible strategies as outlined by the British Columbia Ministry of Education (1997):

_____Acting it out	_____Creating a model
_____Drawing a diagram	_____Looking for patterns
_____Guessing and checking	_____Classifying information
_____Making a list, chart, or table	_____Breaking the problem into patterns
_____Working backwards	_____Using logic
_____Doing simpler problems	_____Numbering the steps in the process
_____Other: _____	

Your students generate a class list of their successful strategies for this learning goal, and you or your students post this to classroom bulletin board or to your subject area online collaborative wiki (a website that allows users to add and edit content). As each of your classes for the same subject and for the same level add to this learning wiki, your students have a list of success strategies from which to choose to improve when their present strategy does not work.

Question as Diagnosis

During the class, in small groups and one-on-one you can ask probing questions that allow you to observe the level of the students' thinking (Namibian National Institute for Educational Development, 2003). As you ask "How are plants and animals similar?" (a higher level thinking question), you listen for the responses such as Jessica's "No idea" (a nonresponse), Takumi's "They are close to my house" (weak response), and Sanne's "They both are alive. They need air and water. They give us food to eat" (strong response). You understand from their answers where their present learning is, and you also know the scientific understanding you want them to have. As you think about the possible strategies to help the nonproficient learners, you consider guided questions starting with "What does an animal need to live?" Likewise, you can use an attribute chart with the categories of plants and animals going across and their attributes going down as shown in Figure 3.4. As students check off which attributes plants or animals have, they come to see the differences between plants and animals.

Figure 3.4. Attributes Strategy Chart

(Attributes)	Plants	Animals

Transform "I Can" Statements Into Learning Solutions

Another tool in your diagnostic repertoire that conveys clearly your analysis of the students' work can be modified "I can" standards-based statements (the skills or knowledge that students will demonstrate—they are worded from a student's view point of "I can"). As you examine students' work, you can think of the success strategies that you and your teaching team have identified for the standard. For example, you take the "I can" learning statements and add particular strategies the students can use to close their writing learning gap in your beginning French high school class, such as the following.

_____ I can conjugate present-tense verbs by: looking at the verb chart; studying the online present tense verb practice; doing peer flash cards; or _____.

_____ I can use the correct adjective form with a noun by: reviewing the noun-adjective chart; doing the adjective-noun practice; checking my answers against the key and looking at the explanations; or _____.

_____ I can select the appropriate verbs for the topic by: looking at the topical vocabulary sheet; brainstorming with another student; looking in the textbook to find at least five topical verbs; or _____.

Analyze Through Exemplars

Students self-analyze the quality of their work when they compare it to an exemplar and then identify what they need to do to improve their learning. For example, as a middle school life careers teacher, you ask your students to compare their work with an exemplar of a stuffed pillow; they are to indicate on a reaction form (shown in Figure 3.5) what the similarities are and what the differences are from the exemplar. In addition, you ask them to indicate if they know how to improve their work or if they need assistance.

Figure 3.5. Exemplary Reaction Form

Exemplary Reaction

The similarities between my work and the exemplar are:

The differences between my work and the exemplar are:

I can make the changes in my work by:

Or

I would like assistance in:

Improve by Using Assessment Tools

Pupils can peer or self-assess, identify their learning strengths and their learning gaps, and have specific direction for improvement if the assessment tool such as a rubric, a rating scale, or a checklist has more than general statements such as "Compares countries." When an assessment tool indicates "Compares the similarities between two countries using three different aspects such as economics, geography, history, diversity, or culture," the students can easily discern what they have in their work already and what are the areas they need to include that they have not. Some students may find it beneficial to highlight the critical term in the rubric and then highlight where the evidence of that term occurs in their work.

Learn Improvement Strategies from Other Students

Learners write up their own goals for improvement in their improvement log after finishing an assignment. Listen as the students explain what areas they need to improve in and how they will improve. For example, Lori, a student in your high school speech class reflects and identifies that she needs to have more eye contact, slow down, and use visuals more effectively. As she thinks of other students who have given speeches, she realizes that she can having more eye contact by looking up after each sentence as Tiffany has done. She also has learned from Alicia that she can use big and easily understandable visuals to improve her communication. Lori's next speech will demonstrate if her diagnosis and own feedback helped her to be more successful in speech giving.

Summary

- ◆ Diagnosis involves both an analysis of the students' assessment and a decision about effective strategies to move the students forward.

- ◆ Effective diagnosis starts with a standard's focus but also includes an understanding of prerequisites, misconceptions, scaffolds, and data triangulation.

- ◆ There are many strategies to diagnose students.

4

Formative Assessment: Feedback for Moving Forward in Student Learning

Overview

- Setting the Stage
- Questions
- Introduction
- Feedback Characteristics
- Feedback Types
- Feedback Groupings within the Classroom

- Student Selection of Their Own Feedback
- Feedback Opportunities and Schedules
- Students Assessment of Class Feedback
- Feedback Time for Improvement
- Summary

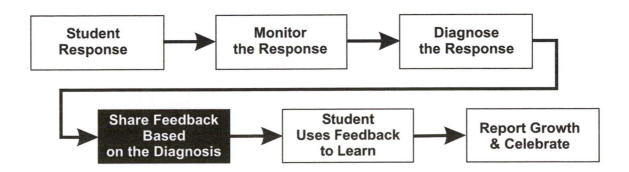

Setting the Stage

Mr. Bacon, the girls' basketball coach, observes Leona during each practice. As he watches her, he identifies a specific problem and thinks about how to remedy the problem. He stops her and explains a layup problem to her. He gives her very specific instructions as to how to improve. He demonstrates the exact action he wants. She practices the movement until she can do it well. The coach realizes that daily direct feedback is the key to Leona's growth. He does not wait until the "big game" to suggest ways for her to improve.

Questions

♦ How do you give feedback to students so they know how they can improve in the standard?

♦ How do you encourage standards-based peer feedback and self-feedback during the class?

♦ How do you build in feedback opportunities?

♦ How can you evaluate the feedback you give to students?

Introduction

As the preceding diagram shows, you have moved from providing the students classroom experiences, observing their work, and diagnosing their work, and, in this part of the formative assessment cycle, you or your students offer specific feedback that can result in improved learning within this lesson or unit. Instead of dwelling on what went wrong, you concentrate on what strategies can move the students forward.

Formative feedback is "the most powerful single moderator in the enhancement of achievement" (Hattie & Jaeger, 1998). Feedback is formative if it leads to improved student learning (Black & Wiliam, 1998; Wiggins, 1998). Tomlinson and McTighe (2006) verify that feedback is formative by asking: "Can the learners tell specifically from the given feedback what they have done well and what they could do next time to improve? If not, the feedback is not specific or understandable enough for the learner" (p. 78).

Feedback serves the purpose of preventing students from reinforcing the same errors and therefore making those errors part of the students' mental strategies (Willis, 2006). Hunter (1982) compares new learning to wet cement. Without appropriate feedback, a mistake at the beginning of the learning can have a long-lasting consequence that is hard for the students to eradicate.

Students are more receptive to your feedback when they understand the standard that they are to learn or do, and they understand the high quality expected of them. When they have seen or even helped create the rubric or checklist on which the feedback is based, they can better comprehend the comments. When students are clear about the learning target and they know that you and their classmates are helping them to achieve it, they feel more motivated to improve (McTighe, & O'Connor, 2006).

Tunstall and Gipps (1996) report that feedback is either descriptive (what the student is doing or saying) or evaluative (judging the standards-based learning). In addition, students prefer descriptive feedback as evaluative feedback may seem like a "put-down" to them.

When your students respond through speaking, doing, producing, or answering on tests, their responses are either correct or incorrect or incomplete. Formative assessment focuses on helping students to expand on the learning if they are correct or to use questions to help the students to understand the answer as Chin (2006) shows in Figure 4.1.

Figure 4.1. Correct or Incorrect Student Response

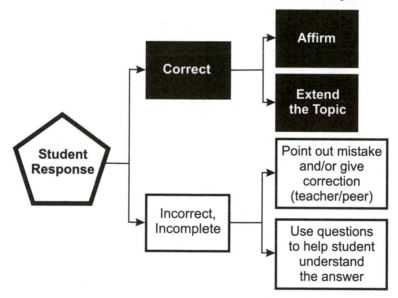

Your students are traveling along a thinking road. They feel that they are heading to a certain standards-based destination only to find out, at the end, that they are on the wrong learning road that has lead them far away from the standards-based destination. Your constant feedback can help them keep on the appropriate standards-based learning road; you assist them from the side. If you put up formative assessment road signs such as the standards, preassessments, and formative feedback, the students can give feedback to others on their standard's progress and can give themselves feedback so they can successfully travel to their learning destination of doing well on the post-assessment. Figure 4.2 illustrates this road.

Figure 4.2.

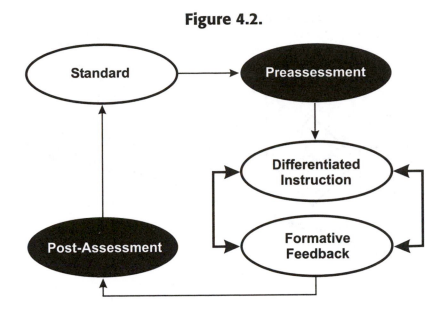

You, other students, the students themselves, or someone outside the classroom can give your students standards feedback. The person gives the feedback to the whole class, small group, or on an individual basis although it benefits the individual student most when the feedback is differentiated. Student feedback focuses exclusively on standards-based classwork or homework. Usually feedback is given through an oral, a written, a nonverbal or a technology method. Furthermore, feedback can be spontaneous or structured. Your feedback can cover all of a particular standards-based assignment or only cover a specific part of it. In addition, feedback can be teacher-directed or focused on the students' own suggestions for improvement (Hall & Burke, 2003).

Assessment for learning fosters student motivation by emphasizing students' progress in a standard; such assessment does not focus on failure. In addition, students are compared to their own progress, not to the progress of their peers. Furthermore, students feel more confident as they can see small steps of success through your feedback. They are more willing to attempt more difficult learning when they are sure that they will receive feedback as they proceed. (Hounsell, 2003).

Feedback is part of a reiterative spiral loop in which students do standards-based work, they receive feedback for improvement, they rework something or proceed to a higher level of it, and receive more feedback so that they can be successful in the standard at the proficient or higher level. Figure 4.3 depicts this cycle.

Figure 4.3. Feedback Cycle

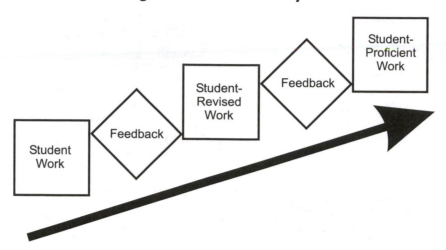

Feedback Characteristics

All feedback generally has the same characteristics (Black & Wiliam, 1998; Heritage, 2007b; Stiggins, 2007b)

- It is standard task specific: Relates the student's work to the standard-based performance task with a sentence such as "You showed how several historical events are connected." Avoids nontask statements such as "Your handwriting was very neat"; avoids comparing to other students with statements such as "The rest of the class understood this"; and avoids personal statements of "I liked..."

- It focuses on the critical aspects of learning: Focuses on two to three critical feedback points at a time. Students can usually accept one or two criticisms, but they may emotionally "shut down" if they hear more. Avoids the tendency of red pen corrections covering every inch of the student's paper.

- It has a descriptive, not evaluative, tone: Is descriptive, "In this paper you used eight different key vocabulary terms" or asks neutral questions such as "How else might you explain the results of this experiment?" Avoids a judgmental tone such as "How could you have ever made so many errors?"

- It is immediate or timely: Gives the feedback as soon after the performance task as possible; the longer the delay, the less meaningful the feedback.

- It is clear and direct: Succinctly communicates the strength or the gap to the students such as "You know your 'five' multiplication tables. Let's see how you can regroup these to show how many trips of five people in a car it will take to transport twenty people."

♦ It provides concrete suggestions for improvement: Avoids vague phrases such as "the quality" or "in general"; avoids general instructional terms such as "Work harder," "Be more thoughtful," and "Include better examples," which are not specific enough to help students.

♦ It is constructive: Concentrates on what the student can do to improve, such as "Follow the one topic and one example rule." Does not concentrate on the negatives of the student work such as "Look at how poorly you wrote this paragraph!"

♦ It is realistic: Suggests a small manageable change rather than a large complex one that the students cannot envision. "Write a better research paper" may be too big a concept for students to grasp, but "state your position on the topic in the thesis statement" is something the students can understand and can do.

♦ It is ongoing: You realize that the more feedback you give students, they better they know how to improve.

♦ It allows for students' own feedback: Asks the students what they felt went well or needs to be improved on.

♦ It asks for students' commitment to change: Helps the students to move from knowing about the need to change to figuring out how to make it happen.

If you give students a grade on a piece of work and also include written comments for improvements, they will not look at the written feedback that you give them for improvement (Butler, 1988). The grade literally cancels out any comments. It is better to only include feedback and not include a grade. An alternative strategy involves only giving a grade once students reach the proficient level.

Feedback can be divided into class, small group, and individual within class groupings as shown by Figure 4.4 (Jefferson Parish Public Schools, n.d.; Lipton & Wellman, 1998; Primary National Strategy, 2004).

Figure 4.4. Feedback to Class, Small Group, or Individual

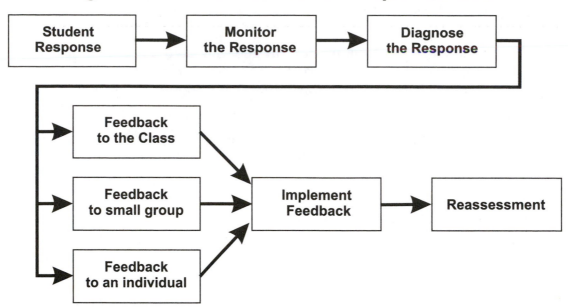

- ◆ Accept the students' difficulty in the learning and share that you want to help them. Examples: "I know you are struggling with this. I'm here to help you," or "The first time you encounter a new idea it can be a challenge. Let's work through this together."

- ◆ Focus the students on the learning purpose with statements. Examples: "We are learning to...," "Let's reexamine what you are to do for this learning task," or "What's our big goal?"

- ◆ Remind students of the high quality of the standards-based learning expected of them through rubrics, numeric scales, and exemplars. Examples: "What does success look like in this project?," "Let's see what this looks like in the exemplar," "What do you have to include in order to do this goal well?," and "How would you rate your work on this scale?"

- ◆ Paraphrase students' responses to help them clarify their thinking with statements. Examples: "How can you say that in other words?," "What examples can you give for that?," "Tell some more about...," and "How did you determine that?"

- ◆ Scaffold the students' learning as they start their work or during their work in progress. Examples: "Let's look at another example," "What will happen if you use the 1-3-1 paragraph model?," and "We can break this problem down by..."

Deliver these statements or questions in a caring and nurturing tone or at least a neutral tone instead of a judgmental or criticizing tone.

To verify that the students have understood your feedback, ask the students to summarize the feedback. Additionally, if you have not provided specific strategies for improvement, ask them how they will implement the changes. After sharing the improvement suggestions, give the students about 10 minutes to read the suggestions and begin to make the changes. For example, your feedback to one of your students, Kate, focuses on indicating the success within the standard, indicating areas for improvement, giving suggestions for the improvement and then having Kate make the corrections. Ask Kate to explain the areas of improvement and your suggestions to verify that she has understood them.

Feedback Types

Formative feedback can be delivered in several different types. In addition to the usual oral and written feedback, there can be nonverbal feedback such as a gesture or motion, and technology feedback such as virtual feedback in a written format (e-mail, part of an online learning system, blog, wiki), in an oral format (podcast) and nonverbal (iMovies).

Hawk and Hill (2001) report that written and oral feedback, each has its own advantages and disadvantages. Figure 4.5 enlarges on their work.

Figure 4.5. Feedback Types

Written Feedback	Oral Feedback	Nonverbal	Technology
Advantages			
• Can be referred to frequently • Is a record of it • Is a more deliberate response because it is not spontaneous • Some students prefer written responses	• Is spontaneous • Can promote a dialogue between student and teacher • Some students prefer oral feedback	• Spontaneous and neutral • Easy to understand • Is silent so that others do not hear it • Some students prefer motion feedback	• Often instantaneous results and feedback • Often a record of the feedback over time
Disadvantages			
• Handwriting may be difficult to read • Takes more time • Students may not understand the feedback	• Easy to forget • No record of it • Students may not understand the feedback	• Easy to forget • No record of it • Students may not understand the feedback. • May work better with application or lower levels of thinking	• Need ready access to technology

Give Written Feedback

Written feedback can be delivered through the use of a checklist or focused rubric that contains specific skills. Check the missing or incomplete skill and add what students can concretely do to improve.

The report card comment process provides another strategy to deliver written feedback. Most report card systems have a bank of comments from which you can choose. You can facilitate written feedback for your students by developing your district, school, team, or your own word-processed bank of comments that has (1) the standard or standard goal; (2) the possible errors, misconceptions, lack of understanding, or lack of logical follow-through that students might make or have in this unit; and (3) several suggestions or remediations for those common errors and misconceptions. By developing this list based on the work that past students have done, you, your team, school, or district create a "best-practice" list of comments. You can all keep these comments in a collaborative online environment such as a wiki or an online class management system such as Blackboard. When students digitally hand in their work, you insert your comments from your bank in bold typeface into their work. When students redo their work, look at your bold comments and see if the students have improved based on your comments. If the students implement your strategy or strategy and still show no improvement, suggest another strategy. Likewise, your team can develop a "praise with reason bank" in which you identify the specific positives for this standard-based learning task.

For the Teachers of English to Speakers of Other Languages (2007) standard of "using English to communicate in social settings," you might identify, for example, that your student, Catalina, does not speak fluently about a topic, and in particular, she does not know how to talk about a picture. Look at your master list of suggestions for improving speaking about a picture, copy some items, offer her some suggestions for improvement, and give her a choice as shown in Figure 4.6.

Figure 4.6. Speaking Feedback From Master-List Feedback Bank

Using English to Communicate in Social Settings

Speaking about the City

Using a visual

Suggestions

♦ Start at the left top part of the picture and tell everything you see happening in the picture. Then move across the picture as if you are reading it.

♦ Look a the picture: ask and answer questions (based on the questions' words) for each object or person that you see.

♦ Pick a person or an object, tell all you know about it (describe the person's physical appearance, their clothing, location, action), and tell about a possible problem with several details. Then tell about another person or

As the students work through the standard goal, you, your team, school, or district create a digital list of the students' faulty logic, misunderstandings, misconceptions, lack of knowledge, or frequent problems. After you have observed students, analyzed their learning gaps, and identified the learning stumbling blocks, you add specific suggestions for improvement for each area and hand this list to the class so they can grow academically. This list grows dynamically from class to class, semester to semester, and year to year. Constructive feedback from a small group, peer, or self-review of students' work can become part of this master list.

Provide Oral Feedback

When you give students oral feedback, there can be a dialogue between you and the student (Cotton, 1988). Students can ask for clarification or can pose an alternative improvement. Chapin, O'Connor, & Anderson (2003) report that elementary math teachers often exemplify using oral feedback to help students expand their learning. One teacher gives her students polygons sets to sort. Within sets there are many different sizes and kinds of triangles made of different colors. As the students sort, she asks her students to justify their categorizations. She asks students if they agree or disagree with the previous explanation and to tell why. She shows her students a triangle with its tip pointing down and asks if it is a triangle. She helps them to realize that polygons can be in different positions and still be the same polygon type.

Use Nonverbal Feedback

A third form of feedback consists of nonverbal feedback to help the students improve in their learning. The nonverbal feedback may be one that the teacher has selected or one that the class has decided on; teachers and students can use it frequently in the class. These nonverbal cues communicate more than just lower-level thinking. As an elementary choir teacher listens to her choir practice, she uses hand gestures to indicate when a sound should be louder (the palm of her hand goes up) or longer (her fingers pull farther and farther apart). A middle school physical education teacher points to her wrist to remind her players to use the correct wrist motion in making a foul line shot as she observes them. When a business teacher reads the first paragraph of a business persuasion letter, he waves his hand to say in his Canadian fashion, "A, Ira!," (**A**ttention, **I**nterest, **R**educe resistance, and **A**ction) to help the student examine which part of the letter is missing.

Employ Technology-Based Feedback

Harness the power of technology to give formative feedback to your students. Talk with your librarian or technology specialist for assistance in learning more about these helpful feedback technologies. Your students can also help you. As you create an online test such as one in Blackboard or ProProfs, you create an explanation of the correct answer. When your students see the correct answer, they also can see the reason for the answer so that they can improve. Likewise, students can have online access through a class website, a blog (an online discussion area), or a wiki (an online collaborative knowledge-building area) to an exemplar that they can use to compare their work to. For example, when students finish their comparison concept map of the rise and fall of supernations; they compare their maps to the exemplar one. Also, students ask each other for help or help each other through a blog or wiki; social studies students may ask students in other fourth-grade classes to help them in brainstorming information about local houses and buildings as they create living history presentations. In addition, you can have mini-Power Point presentations or YouTube videos that give scaffolded, detailed feedback; you or your students can find or create these detailed explanations that guide the learners through a particular process such as dividing fractions.

Feedback Groupings within the Classroom

Each major type of feedback, written, oral, nonverbal, and technology-based can be delivered in the various instructional groupings from whole class to the individual as illustrated in Figure 4.7.

Figure 4.7. Feedback Class Groupings and Feedback Types

	Oral	Written	Nonverbal	Technology-Based
Whole Class				
Small Group				
Pairs				
Individual				

Use Whole Class Feedback

When teachers give whole class feedback, they effectively use classroom time because they are giving feedback to the largest number of students at once (Hounsell, 2003). Following Hounsell's logic, first give whole-class feedback, then small group, next pairs, and lastly individual feedback to be effective in the classroom. Use the broadest brush stroke to help as many students at once and then change to progressively smaller brushes until your feedback gets to each individual, just as a painter starts with the biggest brush in painting a room. For example, as you are reading your third-period class math exit papers that focus on the learning task, you realize that almost all of your students state that they are still unsure of how to use models to make decisions. Decide what specific feedback will benefit the majority of the class and then give the feedback to the whole class.

Look at the Traffic Light Feedback

Students can use a "traffic light" marker system so that you can give more directed feedback (Black, Harrison, Lee, Marshall, & Wiliam, 2002). For example, at the beginning of your math class, you give the answers to the previous night's homework and show the process. Students check their homework against your answers. They use the traffic light system to allow you to give them better feedback. They use a yellow marker if they made a careless mistake such as reversing numbers or forgetting to carry. They use a red marker if they are still confused or are struggling with the concept. As you glance over the marked up homework papers, you can focus in on those students who need your detailed feedback, group these students, and then provide directed feedback. While you work with those students who lack an understanding of the standard's concept (the red students), you ask the other students to do practice problems for avoiding careless mistakes (the yellow students).

Focus on Key Aspects of the Goal

You might focus your feedback and your students' attention on a specific area of the standard in which they are doing less than proficient work. For example, before the science lab, you announce to the students that you are going to concentrate on assessing their hypothesis statements and their proving or disproving of it as you examine their lab reports. As you read the digital lab reports, word process by cutting and pasting a list of the positive ways in which students treat the hypothesis (you can quote these directly) and a list of the areas that need improvement (a paraphrase from a particular student). During the next class, go over these strengths and the areas that need improvement in writing and testing a hypothesis. The class suggests strategies for improvement, and you propose some. Inform students that you will also examine the next lab for their hypothesis statements.

Complete a Class Gallery Walk

A modified gallery walk enables students to get feedback from their peers (Hounsell, 2003). Each student posts his or her work around the room as in an art gallery. The students circulate, read each other's work, and leave a sticky note with one specific praise and one to two specific suggestions for improvement based on your rating scale. The students end with many positives and many ways in which to improve their work based on the standard. Also, the students can do this gallery walk virtually through a blog, wiki, or classroom management system. Decide whether to give additional feedback to the whole class, a group of students or individuals based on certain learning patterns that may have emerged.

Examine an Exemplar

Students can do their own work, compare it against an exemplar, and then revise their own work. For example, a business teacher, Mr. Soderholm has his students word process a persuasion letter for homework. When they come into the class with their homework, he gives them a model or exemplar written answer for the homework letter. As they compare their own letters with the model letter, they write in the margin of their own letters what they now will do to improve their letters. The students offer great self-reflections such as "They started off by really getting their attention. I just made a general statement; I'll use a hook like they did." He allows his students time to redo their letters and then they hand in their improved work.

Show the Class Weekly Standard Average

By using technology, you can show students their progress and more importantly, provide feedback on how to improve. If one of the critical aspects of your school's goals is for your students to develop writing fluency, you can time how many words the students write for different prompts such as "How does reality interfere with your dreams?" during the same number of minutes each day such as eight minutes. At the end of the time, they count the number of words in the second sentence and multiply it by the total number of completed lines. For example, Pablo counts the 10 words in the second line, and he counts the total number of completed lines, which is 12. His writing fluency score is 10×12 or 120. He records the word tally in his writing log for that day.

Give the students another brief activity to do as you go around the room and record their scores. Glance at their papers to see if they have written real, not nonsense, words. Enter their numbers in the classroom desktop computer's writing fluency spreadsheet or on the spreadsheet in a PDA or tablet computer. The computer calculates and graphs the class average.

Project the spreadsheet image to show the students the average class tally for that day without showing any individual tallies (as shown in Figure 4.8); talk about whether the class increased from the last time. Although this assessment does not focus on the individual, each individual will automatically compare the class average with his or her own. By asking students who scored above the class tally average to share what strategy they used, everyone in the classroom can learn new strategies to become fluent in writing. You may post the cumulative class average graph for each week and the list of suggestions for writing more fluently in the classroom and on the class website.

Figure 4.8. Writing Fluency: Words in 8 Minutes

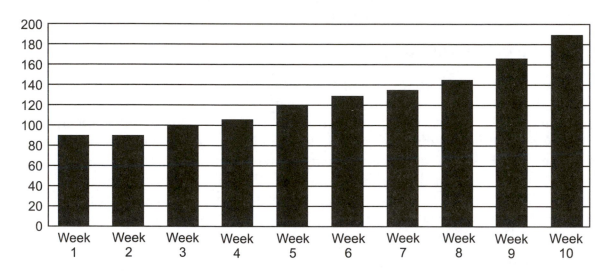

Use Digital Student Exemplars for Feedback

As you walk around the room and see numerous students having difficulty with a classroom learning goal, you find students who are doing exemplary work and take digital pictures with your camera of that work to use during the next class. For example, take a picture of your science students' work of a diagram and an explanation of an atom. In your elementary music class, take pictures of students doing the correct fingering for a recorder. The next day use these digital exemplars to provide formative feedback to those students who are not yet proficient. Ask questions such as, "How does this student work show...?" or "Where is the student's left finger?" A variation is for you to put exemplary work under a document camera when you notice numerous students having difficulty in their learning. Again ask questions to help scaffold their learning so the students can be successful.

Small Group

Once you have given whole class feedback, focus on organizing the class into groups that can give each other feedback and into small groups that you target for specific feedback. Spend time in class helping students understand how to give feedback through highly structured standards-based nonjudgmental ways. The students will need these skills in a collaborative work environment. For the targeted small groups, group students based on their pretest or in class formative assessments so that you can concentrate on a specific learning gap.

Provide Mini-Fishbowl Feedback

When students work in pairs, a third student can act as an observer and feedback giver. For example, students in your high school English as other language class use this mini-fishbowl strategy when they role play a conversation such as a police officer interviewing a person about a car accident. Two students role-play; Nanami is the police officer, and Lautaro is the driver of the car involved in the accident. The third person, Vicente, listens and uses a checklist. After the short role-play, Vicente gives feedback to each speaker according to forms that you made. He informs Nanami, "You asked five different questions. You did not ask 'Where' or 'How.' What 'How' question you can ask?" Vincente uses your list of helpful written prompts for each question word.

Create Small Group Feedback Log

A small group can present its status to you in several ways, and you can give them feedback.

Each group keeps a cumulative log of what the group has done each day by checking off those learning tasks they have done; they show you evidence of their having accomplished the standard-based learning tasks. In addition, they share with you any concerns or problems. Figure 4.9 shows a sample form. Each group can give these group-learning logs to you physically, or they can put them online in a class management system or a blog. You read these and then have a conference with the group in which you give them constructive feedback so that they can progress in the standard. In addition, you may prefer to assess the students' learning orally by asking each group member a different question about the topic. You might notice that one group is struggling with comparing two newspaper stories about the same event. Ask them to do a Who-What-Where-When-Why and position chart to see the differences in the articles.

Figure 4.9. Small Group Feedback Log

Group Name: The Tigers					
Group Purpose:					
Day	Today's Action Plan for the Standard-Based Experience	Successes	Evidence of Success	Concerns, Questions, Problems	Tomorrow's Action Plan

Think-Pair-Share on Individual Goals

After a few days on a new unit, your students do a think-pair-share on what their individual goals were, what strategies they have found successful, and what evidence shows their success. Students can share successful strategies with each other and give specific feedback to each other on how to improve in the standard. For example, Peter lets Jackie know that she has copied much of Braque's Cubism style in her painting by using geometric shapes, but her painting would more closely resemble his art by showing several aspects of the object at the same time.

Give Peer Feedback After Completing a Checklist

Students can check off items from a standards-based checklist as they examine each other's work, and they support their statements with examples from their partners' work. When students use these standards-based performance checklists, they look for specific items evident in a student's work; they are not asked to interpret the profound meaning of the work. When the students finish the peer review, they give the checklist to the creator of the work. A middle school English checklist for a persuasive paragraph includes these check points:

Yes or No. If no, give a explanation of how to change it so that it can become a Yes.

☐ Does the first sentence mention the topic to be proved?

Example:_____

☐ Are there three specific examples?

Example:_____

☐ Does each example prove the topic of the paragraph?

Example:_____

☐ Is each example different?

Example:_____

Students can complete these checklists on paper and pencil or do them electronically.

Writing Feedback Model

Many elementary language arts classrooms use a writing feedback model that involves a student reading another student's writing and then stating two things that the reader likes in the writing and one area for improvement. You can modify this to include two things that the student does well in terms of the standard goal and one specific area that could be improved. Another variation is the sandwich approach in which a student gives a positive, an area for improvement, and then another positive. If the student offering the feedback has a strategy that he or she uses, he or she suggests it as another possible strategy.

Identify Strategies and Supply Missing Ones

Students can be assigned not to judge another student's work but to identify what exists in that student's work and to provide examples of what is missing. Tuttle (2004) describes the process for improving descriptive writing. In a high school English class, each student writes a descriptive passage about a shown visual. Then students exchange papers. Next, they follow directions on a sheet that has them make a shape around any words that identify a certain type of description:

Category = Shape

color words = rectangle

weight words = oval

size words = circle

shape words = triangle

direction words = arrow

After the reviewers have made the shapes on the paper, they write down how many different examples of each descriptive word category the author includes. In addition, the reviewers create sentences for any descriptive word category that their partners did not use. They return the paper as show in Figure 4.10 to the author. The author looks to see how many shapes he or she has and what specific examples the reviewer has supplied.

Figure 4.10. Peer Descriptive Writing Feedback

The bed has a | pink | sheet on it. On the right side of the bed, there is a | yellow | desk with

three drawers. On top of the desk are two | black | clocks, one is square. In back of the

desk is | green | wallpaper with trees.

	How many	Example for any missing descriptions
Color words (rectangle)	4	
Shape words (triangle)	1	…clocks, one is square and the one is oblong
Weight words (oval)	0	the heavy bed
Direction words (arrow)	3	
Size (circle)	0	the big heavy bed

Have Group Give Specific Feedback

Assign pairs of students to peer review each other. In addition, you may want a small-group peer review in which each group member specifically focuses in one aspect of the rubric, rating scale, or checklist. For example, Jill looks at all the papers from another science group for how well they used a graph to argue their point. If she notices any part is missing, she indicates it and refers to the books' pages that explain it. Franco checks that they have at least four relevant sources and those sources are in American Psychological Association (APA) format; if not, he supplies hints or suggestions for their improvement. Beatriz verifies that they have three different science real-world examples; she does a web check, creates a concept map to determine if they are different, and provides advice if they do not have three different real-world examples. Aoi examines their papers for their scientific process, and she sends back a list of missing or incomplete components and a reference to the class exemplar.

One-On-One or Self-Feedback

After you have used whole-class and small-group feedback, either provide one-on-one feedback with individual students, or have the students give themselves feedback. Students can develop the ability to metacognate and to offer themselves feedback after you have helped them gradually develop this skill.

One-on-One Talk

As you have a one-on-one talk with a student you can listen to see if the student uses your formative feedback to arrive at a higher level of thinking.

Mr. Brown, a middle school science teacher, has asked each student to design an original experiment and one of his students, Viki, conferences with him after getting his feedback.

Viki: I've read your feedback. You suggested that I word my science experiment in the form of a hypothesis. Do you mean something like, "There are flies in school."?

Mr. Brown: Viki, what are you interested in finding out about flies?

Viki: Your room seems to have lotsa flies. Why is that?

Mr. Brown: You've identified a topic—the number of flies. And, you are interested in it. How might you word your hypothesis statement so that you can prove it or disprove it?

Viki: You mean like, "There are many flies in Mr. Brown's classroom."?

Mr. Brown: What evidence might you use to prove or disprove that statement?

Viki: Um. I guess I better change it to something that I can prove. Maybe, "Mr. Brown's classroom has more flies than any other classroom in our school."

Add Feedback to Students' Journals

As you read a student's learning log, journal entries, or reflections, write your formative feedback comments. Ask your students to create two columns in their logs. They write in the first column, and you respond with formative feedback in the second. Offer "feed-forward" formative comments for a garden math project as indicated in Figure 4.11.

Figure 4.11. Student Learning Log Feedback

My Thoughts	Teacher's Comments
4/4 It is hard to plan out the class garden. We have to figure out how much total ground we have, how much space each plant needs, and how many plants to plant. We also have to think about what plants could be good neighbors.	Show each different plant by a different colored block that is the same size that the plant needs. For example, a red radish block would be 6 inches (space between each seed in a row) by 8 inches (distance between the rows of the same plant). Make these blocks for each plant type and then plan out your garden using your manipulatives.

Offer Feedback through Coupons and Special Cards

A world language teacher, Miss Viders, implements a system of coupons in which she gives out based on classroom language use (Tuttle, 2007g). She gives a one-point coupon to represent a student identifying a vocabulary item such as "window" or doing a grammar item such as the "I" form of the verb. A two-point coupon represents asking or answering a basic question such as "Where do you live?" through speaking or writing. A three-point coupon represents the student saying or writing two consecutive sentences. A 20-point coupon indicates that the student has read, listened, or watched some information, and responds by speaking or writing 10 different consecutive sentences or 10 different consecutive questions about the topic. The students know that by the end of the month they are to have at least 120 points.

As Miss Viders hands out one- or two-point coupons, she also hands out special cards that provide specific feedback on improving a student's language use. For example, one special card says "Describe what a person looks like physically (1) with personal adjectives such as tall and thin, and (2) what the person is wearing such as shirt and shoes," while another says, "Say five actions you do in your kitchen such as cook and eat." Through this feedback, the students can increase the number of sentences they say and write in the class.

Analyze Weekly Scores

Have students analyze their own scores on a weekly basis to see their progress and then make decisions about changing their learning strategy to improve (Tuttle, 2004). For example, if you give a vocabulary quiz each week in social studies, have the students graph their scores in a computer spreadsheet on their laptop or in the computer lab. Create a vocabulary score spreadsheet template for them and distribute it to their laptops or lab computer stations. If you give the quiz on Friday, return it on Monday; they may take it online and get the results back instantly. On the quiz, they indicate what strategy they used to learn the words; they may not use "memorized." The students enter the score for that quiz into the spreadsheet, and the computer generates the graph of their learning; a sample student's spreadsheet is shown in Figure 4.12. If the students score above an 80, they continue with their present vocabulary strategy. If they score below an 80, then they are to select from a list of alternative vocabulary learning strategies that the class generated. They try that strategy out for the next two weeks to see if their weekly score increases. Because you have also entered their scores in your grade book or spreadsheet, you can ask students who scored below 80 what new strategy they are going to use to improve.

Figure 4.12. Vocabulary Score over Time

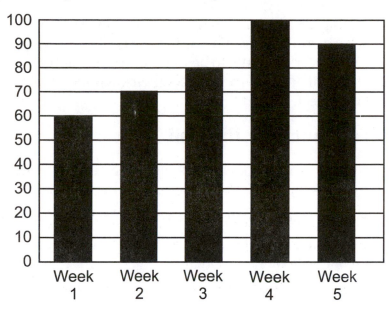

Check Against Your Rating

Students can develop their ability to be better self-assessors by first assessing other students' work. You can use a physical or digital binder in which you have samples of student work from past years (Willis, 2006). Students assess a particular work and then compare their assessments to your assessment of the same work that is in the binder. These samples will be on the same general topics that are in the present unit, but they will not be identical. For example, last year's literary analysis of two poems might have focused on the theme of courage in adversity, whereas this year your students compare a poem and a short story on the theme of being true to oneself. As students become better self-assessors, they can better analyze their work and give themselves more effective feedback.

Self-Assess Their Goals

If you believe that students are to be lifelong learners, they have to be able to self-assess (Black & Wiliam, 1998). To help your students become more self-directed, they make a list of their personal goals for this standard. They identify what they want to be able to know or do by the end of the unit or semester. At various points during the unit, ask the students to self-assess their progress in their goals and to indicate what they can do to progress more. For example, Jessica decides that she wants to explore the art of other cultures as part of the multicultural standard for art, so she will study two pieces of art from each continent before the semester ends. As she shares her goal with you, ask her how she will indicate what she is learning about the other cultures through the art.

Student Selection of Their Own Feedback

Students can help give feedback to others, and they can select how they want their own feedback given. Because one of the goals of each subject is to develop lifelong learners, empower students to be more in control of their learning. Over a series of lessons, students can learn to select their own feedback so that they can grow more in your subject.

Select Their Feedback for the Unit

At the beginning of a unit, have students indicate how they would like to receive feedback (Hounsell, 2005). The students can check as many as they prefer.

- ☐ Written feedback ("Read these comments.")

- ☐ Oral feedback ("Huan, to improve you will think about what other similar heat reaction experiments we have done.)

- ☐ Student-Teacher mini-conference ("Let's meet for a few minutes and talk about it."

- ☐ Want errors or problems specifically identified ("You are missing your third example.")

- ☐ Want errors or problems generally identified ("Look in this paragraph for your development problem.")

- ☐ Want areas and general directions for improvement "You are missing the third example, check your second paragraph."

- ☐ Want errors and specific strategies for improvements ("You are missing the third example; use the 1-3-1 rule.")

- ☐ From another student ("Juan, how did I score against the rubric?")

Select Rubric Part for Detailed Feedback

After the students have completed the self-assessment and made comments, they circle one part of the rubric for you to focus on. For example, a high school music student, Fatma, works on the standard of the relationship of music to other disciplines. She looks at the three rubric categories of identifying a musical development, identifying a cultural or historical event, and demonstrating the connection between the music and the culture/history through examples. This student circles the last category because she wants more focused feedback on how well she connects the music with the culture/history. Although you assess the other categories, spend more time on giving concrete feedback on the student-selected category so she can become proficient.

Feedback Opportunities and Schedules

When you build in small group, peer, and individual work within the class period, you have time to work with individuals or small groups. As the instructional leader for the classroom, decide how to build more feedback opportunities into the curriculum. In the big-to-small strategy, break big assignments into smaller parts and provide brief feedback on these smaller parts. For example, as an elementary social studies teacher, you can divide the major "compare two countries" project into these four parts: identify the countries and the categories for the comparisons; show the research and notes; organize to show the similarities; and create the Power Point presentation (Figure 4.13). The more feedback you provide to students while they are doing each part of the project, they more likely they are to be able to successfully demonstrate the particular goal of the standard.

Figure 4.13. Project Feedback Opportunities

Comparison countries project: Whole project with one final assessment or sections each with an assessment					
Project A with no feedback	—	—	—	—	Assessment	Low or high quality work?
Project B with multiple feedbacks	Identification of countries and categories •Listing assessment	Research and notes •Outline assessment	Organization to show similarities •Venn diagram assessment	Creation of presentation •Self-assessment checklist	Assessment	High quality work!

Decide to create a feedback schedule (Hounsell, 2003). For example, as an elementary teacher you may give oral feedback to each student in one-half of your class for a week while the other half gets written feedback. The next week you switch to giving more in-depth oral feedback to the individuals in the other half of the class. The first time you meet with the student you guide the student in understanding his or her mistakes and provide probing questions to help him or her figure out how to remedy that learning problem. The next time you meet ask the student what the problem was, what the student was to do, and see if the student has been able to do it.

As part of small-group time, schedule a fixed time to conference with each group. Your time for being with each group changes on a rotational basis as illustrated in Figure 4.14. Your schedule allows time in between each group to record your comments to the group and to get additional materials for students. For example, as a middle school science teacher you rotate from group to group as each group does its plant experiment. You have prepared your feedback for each group from your observations of the previous day. When you give feedback, ask questions such as "What might happen if we put one plant in the closet and the other one on the windowsill? How much does sunlight impact the growth of a plant?"

Figure 4.14. Small Group Rotation Teacher Feedback Time

	10:00–10:05	10:10–10:15	10:20–10:25	10:30–10:35
Day 1—Group	A	B	C	D
Day 2—Group	B	C	D	A
Day 3—Group	C	D	A	B
Day 4—Group	D	A	B	C

Pick a feedback circulation pattern that will guarantee that within several days you will observe and give feedback to each individual student in your class. For example, if you have your classroom desks arranged in a huge semicircle, focus on those students on the left side of the semicircle on Tuesday; on Wednesday, spend time with the students on the right side. Each student has equal access to your feedback; give short, targeted feedback to each student.

By using your pile of students' names on index cards, create another pattern of scheduling deliberate feedback. Shuffle the cards and then take the top half of the cards and make sure to give standards-based feedback to those students whose names are on the cards during the class period. The next day do the other half. In a similar manner, you may only select five cards at a time so that you talk with five students each day. Within a week you will have given all students meaningful feedback to help them move forward in their learning.

Perhaps you want to leave the feedback schedule to the students. Ask students to schedule when they would like you to talk with them during the period in blocks of three minutes (Figure 4.15). They go to the drop-by-schedule poster and write in their name. For example, you inform the students that at each major step in a project, they are to check in with you, and they can chose when to check in. Students see the sign that has a listing of the times and the different parts of the standards-based project. The students schedule their mini-conferences with you. As the students have their mini-conferences with you, assess their work, praise them for successes, identify areas for improvement or areas that have not been done yet, and offer specific suggestions or ask them for suggestions for improvement.

Figure 4.15. Student Choice Check-in Schedule

Design a Future City Project Standard: People, Places, and Environments Schedule at 3 minute intervals such as 2:03, 2:06, 2:09, 2:12, 2:15, etc.						
Period 3 2:00– 2:40	City infrastruc-ture identification Jan. 14–15	Possible energy reources—advantage/ disadvantage Jan. 16–17	Design the city Jan. 18–23	Essay explaining your design and reasons Jan. 24–25	Peer or expert assessment/ Changes Jan. 28–29	Self-Assessment Jan. 30–31
2:03						
2:06						
2:09						
2:12						
2:15						

Supply Feedback Over Time on One Standard

As previously mentioned in *Record a Standard's Observations Over Time* in chapter 2, you can assess over time the same standard, analyze the results of the state benchmark rubric, and provide feedback so you can help your students' constantly improve in the standard. Continual monitoring, diagnosing, and giving feedback on the same standard, create a model for success as shown in Figure 4.16.

Figure 4.16. Standard Feedback Over Many Weeks

Students Assessment of Class Feedback

Students can complete a form as shown in Figure 4.17 to help you and others know how well the feedback is helping them (Brown, Gibbs, & Glover, 2003):

Figure 4.17. Students Assess Class Feedback

Feedback	Coding: NA = not applicable; 0 = None; 1 = Some; 2 = A lot					
	To the whole class	To me personally	Outside of class	Other students' feedback during group assignment	Peer feedback on my own assignment	Self-assessment on my own assignment
Helped me to understand the standard and goals.						
Helped me know how well I am doing						
Helped me to understand where I am going wrong						
Made it clear what I need to do to improve						
Helped me with subsequent assignments						
Engaged me in revisiting the text and other sources for further study						
Helped me to develop my intellectual skills (problem solving and analysis)						
Allowed me opportunities to revise work or test						
Helped me to understand why I get my grade or mark						

Feedback	Coding: NA = not applicable; 0 = None; 1 = Some; 2 = A lot					
Helped toward the test						
Motivated me to keep going and try harder						

Feedback Time for Improvement

Once you have supplied students with feedback, provide them with the time to reflect on the feedback and then with time to implement the improvements. Without this built-in time, the students may never act on the feedback. When you are having trouble with your car, you take it to a mechanic. How would you feel if the mechanic looked at your car, wrote out what was wrong and then told you to drive away?

Build in feedback time just as a coach builds in practice time. For a smaller goal, you can return the work and have the students immediately make changes. For more complex tasks such as creating a nature trail for a nearby nature area, the students will need more time to think through the feedback and determine how to move forward. When you break tasks down into meaningful blocks, you give your students feedback and give them class time to improve each part before moving on.

Summary

♦ After teachers and students observe and analyze students' work, they are ready to give feedback to move the students forward in their learning.

♦ Numerous traits make feedback more effective for the students such as being timely, constructive, and standards-based.

♦ Feedback can be delivered in oral, written, nonverbal, and technology format.

♦ Whole-class, small-group, pair, and individual feedback can be given.

♦ You can build in feedback opportunities so that each student frequently receives critical feedback.

♦ Once students receive the feedback, provide time to modify their past work into proficient work.

♦ Formative feedback specifically tells the student how to improve; it is not a general statement such as "Study more."

5

Formative Assessment: Students' Improvement Based on Feedback

Overview

- ◆ Setting the Stage
- ◆ Questions
- ◆ Introduction
- ◆ Proof of Improved Student Learning through Feedback
- ◆ Creation of New Activities or Tests
- ◆ Summary

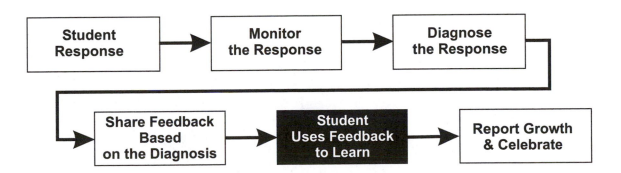

Setting the Stage

Miss Webster, an instrumental teacher, asks her student, Alan, to play a piece. She notices his inability to play a high C, discerns that his problem is with his embouchure, offers him feedback on his mouthpiece placement, then has him practice playing the high C with the new embouchure. Then she wants to see Alan incorporate that technique into the piece. He shows that he can do it. Both Miss Webster and he smile proudly.

Questions

♦ How do students show that they have improved in their standards-based learning based on your, peer, or self-formative feedback?

♦ How do you provide additional tests or assignments?

Introduction

As you have followed the previous standards and formative assessment cycle, you have engaged the students in a learning experience, observed them, diagnosed their strengths and learning gaps, and provided constructive feedback, now you wait for the excitement of seeing their improved learning. You want to know not only that the students have understood the constructive feedback but that they have used it to grow in the standard.

For students to demonstrate their learning, they need time and the scaffolded assistance to jump over the learning gaps that you have identified. Then students can show their growth through what they say, do, produce, their tests, and portfolios. Hunter (1982) uses the analogy that teaching without proof of student learning is like saying that you are selling when no one is buying. Students have "bought" the learning when they have benefited from the standards-based feedback by doing better in their learning as illustrated in Figure 5.1.

Figure 5.1. Feedback Leads to Student Improvement

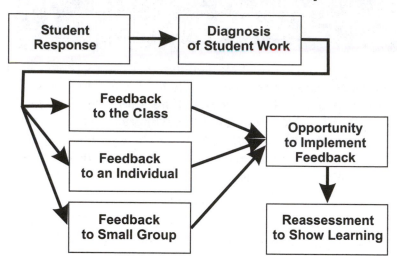

Proof of Students' Improving Their Standards-Based Learning through Feedback

You want to know not only that the students heard the constructive feedback, but that they have used it to move forward in their learning. Students can demonstrate that they have applied your feedback in numerous ways as you show them over a period of time various strategies for self-reflection. The more you can help them to metacognate, the better they will be prepared to be lifelong learners.

Use a Checklist Feedback Form

Learners can use the feedback form as a checklist before turning in their assignment (Science Education Resource Center, 2008). For example, put a plus sign (+) in front of those areas that a social studies student, Ava, has shown proficiency in her document-based question (DBQ) on immigration. After she reads the feedback form that you created and makes her changes, she puts a plus sign (+) for those elements that she can now demonstrate.

Figure 5.2. Plus/Minus Checklist

DBQ Body:		
First Paragraph		
Teacher	**Student**	**Checklist Item**
+	+	Starts the paragraph with a topic sentence
–	+	Bases the topic sentence on the thesis from the introductory paragraph
–	+	Uses multiple documents in this paragraph

Likewise, students can complete their own checklist to indicate what they have done on the checklist and the proof of how they have done it (Project Based Learning Checklists, 2007). A partial elementary science student's checklist about answering questions is displayed in Figure 5.3.

Figure 5.3. Proof of Learning Checklist

Check Off	**Checklist**	**My Proof:**
✓	I made up some of my own questions.	I now have three questions about the sun.
✓	I asked my teacher about things I did not understand.	I asked about our sunlight experiment. Last time I did not understand what I was to do.
✓	I asked other students about things I did not understand.	This time I asked them about rotation.
✓	I looked up things I didn't understand.	I went to the websites listed by my teacher, I did not Google it.

Count and Show Improvements

Your students can have student counters to help them show their learning changes. When two students originally argue the two sides of the science topic, "forest preservation versus housing development," a third student listens, identifies the major points, indicates how many examples were given for each main point in a teacher-provided chart, and reports back to the debaters. The students work on improving their major points with more examples and more specific examples through a graphic organizer. They do their pro–con speeches again, and the third student listens again. The counter reports back on their success and hands in the two charts from both speeches.

Include Improvement through Columns

There are numerous ways in which students summarize the feedback they receive and note the changes they make in their revised document (Science Education Resource Center, 2008). In the first, students summarize their peer's feedback and then show the revised work. For example, a Social Studies student shows both the peer feedback (left side) and her revised work based on the peer feedback (right side) in Figure 5.4.

Figure 5.4. Peer Feedback Leads to Improvement

Feedback That Led to Revisions:	Revised Work:
Gary suggested: Reason for the written language; Specific language group of Karens instead of just groups	Baptist missionaries helped educate people in Burma. To teach people religion and, specifically, to read the Bible, the missionaries had to create a written language for the Karen people because these people only had an oral language.

Another technique is for the students to show their original work along with your comments in one column (left side) and then the changes they made based on the comments (right side) as illustrated in Figure 5.5.

Figure 5.5. Teacher Feedback Leads to Improvements

Original with the Teacher's Comments in Italics	My Changes
A Midsummer Nights' Dream and Don Quixote are about love *(Authors? Also, improve by using a verb other than "are").* In both works the characters do things out of love *(Which characters?)*	Shakespeare's *A Midsummer Nights' Dream* and Cervantes' *Don Quixote* focus on fantasy love. Quixote and Lysander do things out of their love.

In a three-column approach, the students include their own self-review, the peer's review, and then their new thinking about the topic. (Science Education Resource Center, 2008). Figure 5.6 shows the work of a high school art student who has explained which painting, Picasso's *Guernica* or West's *The Death of General Wolfe,* is more realistic.

Figure 5.6. Self and Peer Review Leads to Improvement

My self-review	Peer review	My Comments for Moving Forward More
I identified *Death of General Wolfe* as the more realistic by ♦ Identifying the minute details in the painting such as the bayonet in front of the general. ♦ Seeing that all the figures are focused on the dying General ♦ Observing the depiction of Native Americans as noble savages	♦ Wolfe does include many vivid details. What are some others? ♦ How do the figures focusing on the dying general depict realism? ♦ How does the noble savage portray realism?	I was thinking of realism as the depiction of real things. I now realize that Wolfe also has some nonrealistic things in the picture such as the kneeling Native American who looks like Rodin's *Thinker*.

A final one-column approach is a cover letter in which the students explain how they revised their document in response to the reviews (Science Education Resource Center, 2008). In Miguel's cover memo, which is displayed below, he explains the changes that he made in his negative message letters in his high school business course.

> When I received the feedback, I realized that in my business "bad news" letter, I did not completely follow the pattern of "Buffer, Reasons, Bad News, and Closing"; I did not start with a neutral statement. My letter did not use an indirect approach: I directly said the customer was denied the membership. I needed to soften my approach so that I hide the bad news and do not directly announce it; I need to avoid directly denying the person her membership.

Talk to Teacher or Write in the Journal

Students discuss the feedback with you or in their learning journals to help develop strategies for improvement (Science Education Resource Center, 2008). For example, you have your elementary students do a science experiment to determine if certain leaves are of the same or different type based on their measurements. One of the students, Shay, is not successful in her experiment, and you have written up some questions for Shay to think about:

> Shay: My experiment didn't work. In your reaction, you asked how I had measured the different leaves. I used the metric stick.

Mrs. Lee: Yes, in science class we measure using a metric stick. Please show me how you measure a leaf.

Shay: I hold the meter stick over the leaf and look at where the leaf ends. (She demonstrates.)

Mrs. Lee: Shay, I've notice that you do not put the metric stick on the leaf. Let's see what happens if you do that.

Shay: (puts the meter stick on the leaf and reads the measurement) Wait, this time it is longer!

Mrs. Lee: Shay, which way do you think is more accurate? The meter stick above the leaf or on it?

Shay: On it. I'm going to redo my measurement with putting the meter stick on the leaves.

(A few minutes later)

Shay: Mrs. Lee, look! I've arranged the leaves by their sizes. I have three different piles.

Prove Success of Additional Help, New Strategy, or Learning

Students can demonstrate in numerous ways that they have received additional assistance in their learning and have learned the designated goal.

♦ The learners show that to become proficient in the learning task, they have worked with a peer or other person on the standard goal or have attended a tutoring session (Stiggins, 2004). For example, Sharon, an elementary English as other language student listens to your feedback suggestions for improvement in talking about the post office. You suggest that she practice with another person. Her partner checks off each post office vocabulary word that she uses and lets her know which words she does not use. Sharon practices, shows you her partner's checklist that shows that she can use at least eight post office vocabulary words, and then redoes the oral activity successfully.

♦ In addition, students demonstrate that they have practiced alternative problems, worked on software or a website that allows them to practice the standard, or have taken a practice online test with successful results. For example, as a high school math teacher, you identify Alec's lack of understanding of differentiation on the last calculus assignment. You suggest an online math help site, Math Medic's S.0.S. Math (2007). Alec reads the tutorial, does the practice, and prints out the practice page with his answers. He shows you his practice printout on which he has done well. Then he redoes the calculus assignment.

- In a third strategy, your students demonstrate they have used a different strategy in improving their work by listing their beginning thinking, their reflections, and their new strategy. In your middle school technology education class, you have students in small groups plan out and build a toothpick bridge, analyze the design of all the bridges, watch what happens as the weight is applied to each bridge, and redesign their bridges. However, this time they list what new building strategies they have learned from all the bridge designs and performance and what they are going to do to improve their design. They build their new bridges.

- Furthermore, the learners use digital pictures or screen captures of successive stages of their work based on feedback to show their progress. Middle school social studies students who are doing a city creation simulation take screen shots of various stages in the simulation, and they take a screen shot of their online word-processed reflections about how to improve in the simulation. They present a digital slide show of the purpose of the learning, their actions in the simulation, their reflections based on the reflection form that you created, their new actions, more reflections, and the final stages of their success.

- Also, your learners create iMovies or podcasts to show their new skills. For example, Jacob makes a short movie showing how he used to do the specific soccer skill of kicking a ball, the feedback that he received, and how he has improved in kicking. Many students already know how to take movies with their digital camera, digital camcorder or a cell phone. If not, you can ask your school librarian or technology specialist to help the students.

- In addition, students can use their Blackboard, blog, or wiki online discussion to show the changes in their thinking. For example, a student, Janet, copies the online discussion into a word processor, italicizes her original contributions to the discussion, underlines the feedback from other students that caused her to rethink your position, and bolds her ending statements that show her new position. She adds a reflection on how she enlarged her thinking after thinking about the comments of others.

- Furthermore, your pupils can show graphs of their growth in their learning. They can visually demonstrate their numbers of typed words in a certain time period for business class or the number of additional different connections in their middle school science concept map about birds from their original map. To add more learning power to their graphs, they provide an explanation of what they did to increase in their learning

♦ Class discussions can be excellent opportunities for your students to show their starting view, what they have learned, and their new view of a topic. For example, you start off your high school science class discussion with students writing down their own views and reasons on a topic such as, "bioengineering of plants should be prohibited." Then you stop the discussion periodically for the students to write down the ideas that the class has generated and to compare their ideas in a graphic organizer with the ideas of others. At the end of the class, they re-examine their original ideas and supporting ideas, look at the notes they have taken, study the graphic organizer showing the different points of view that exist, and state their present view and their reasons.

Provide In-depth Analysis and Change

Students do an in-depth analysis of why they got the material incorrect or why they did it incompletely, identify how to do it to proficiently, and revise their work. The British Columbia Ministry of Education (2007) suggests the following specific steps (Figure 5.7) in helping students to work through a problem.

Figure 5.7. Problem Solving Analysis

Problem: _____
Why it was a problem:
_____
How I solved it:
_____
How I will solve future problems:
_____
Other strategies I might use:
_____
What I learned:
_____

Show Change Based on an Exemplar

Students take their own work, compare it to an exemplar, revise it, and show both the original and the revision to you. For example, as the students come into the business class with their direct request business letter that you assigned as homework, give them an exemplar for the homework letter. Ask them to compare their own letters with the exemplar letter. They write in the margin of their letters what they now can do to improve their letters. Allow them time to redo the letters within the class. They pull up their previous word-processed files, make the changes, print them out, and attach them to the original homework and the exemplar. The students have gone from a developing stage to a proficient stage of quality work through learning from an exemplar.

Demonstrate Growth through a Portfolio

Students develop lifelong skills in self-assessment and accountability as they work on and produce their e-portfolios. (Tuttle, 2007a). They select their own assignments as evidence and explain how they are progressing in the standard. Your students are accountable for their own selection of specific work for the standard.

When students select their own evidence and when they revisit their portfolio on a regular basis, they decide if their original evidence is the "best" evidence that they have to demonstrate the learning up to this moment. For example, a middle school science student, James, looks in his portfolio for the standard of scientific inquiry. He reviews his original selection, a water experiment he planned; he looks at the feedback you gave him on this experiment. He thinks about what he has done in the last 10 weeks. He thinks about a new experiment that he not only planned but actually conducted on sound levels in the school. James compares the sound experiment to the rubric for inquiry and sees if he has incorporated your feedback into his new experiment. He realizes that his sound experiment is a stronger demonstration of inquiry so he uses it as his new portfolio example.

Reflections are a critical part of student electronic portfolios or e-portfolios. Students will include insightful reflections in their e-portfolio that show what they have learned and what they still need to learn about the standard. The students have to be able to determine what they did well and what improvements they can make to improve in the future. For example, in the first reflection in Rima's high school English standards portfolio, you read "I liked writing the essay about these two works of literature. Both works of literature were great. I used the theme of love from the list the teacher gave us. For this essay I was told to tell three similarities or three differences and give examples of each. I followed the comparison/contrast essay format that the teacher gave us; I developed my outline using it. I looked over my notes and the class handouts and got the examples from them. It did not take me very long to do. I wrote five paragraphs. I outlined it and then word processed it. I think I did a good job." You realize that nothing in this "reflection" is a real reflection; Rima has simply summarized what she had to do. You give her a reflection model to follow so that she can reveal her thinking and learning more.

When you look at a reflection from another student, Amy, for the same standard, you realize that she has read your and peer feedback and has made changes. "I had trouble deciding whether I wanted to compare or contrast the two works of literature. I did a quick concept map of both and found that I had more complete examples to show their similarities. I could more easily prove the similarities after I changed the theme of "love" to "crazy love." I realized that both authors used humor to show how love can be crazy. This time I listed examples of "crazy love" from each. Next time, I will match up the examples from the literature and show precisely how similar they are, instead of how generally similar they are." Amy clearly reflects her thinking about the standard, and she includes a specific suggestion for future improvements. Figure 5.8 illustrates the importance of avoiding general reflections and using specific reflections.

Figure 5.8. Specific Reflections for Self Growth

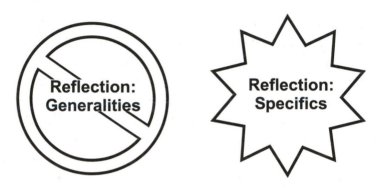

One model to guide students in reflecting on their work for each standard is a modified know, want to know, and learned (KWL) chart that is called "knew, learned, and what to learn" as shown in Figure 5.9. This is a variation on Stiggins (2007a) self-reflection, "what I used to ___; now I ____." Students state what they kne w before about the standard, what they learned about this standard, and what more they want to learn about it. This KLW can be built into the e-portfolio template for each standard so that the students have to deliberately consider these aspects. Their reflections demonstrate their ability to be accountable for their own learning. When Angela writes, "I learned to write better," she either does not know what she learned or she has not learned how to be specific.

Your students only show their standards growth in e-portfolios when they do in-depth reflection.

Figure 5.9. KLW Guided Reflection

Standard 1	My Reflection	
K	**L**	**W**
What I already knew about the standard?	What I learned about it or how I grew in my progress toward the standard?	What I still need to learn about or be able to do in my progress toward the standard
Portfolio Reflection—**K** *What I already knew about Standard 2: Personal Expression,* I had previously learned many poetry terms, written very structured poems, and modeled my poems closely after the poems we did in class.	Portfolio Reflection—**L** *What I learned about this standard:* I learned that I can express a single concept (flower as skyscraper) by using many different poetry elements such as metaphor, images, and word choice. I learned that when I focus several poetry elements on the one purpose, the poem has a stronger message.	Portfolio Reflection—**W** *What I still need to know about this standard:* I want to work more on making more elements of my poem focus on my one single concept so that the poem will communicate my feeling about the topic better. I need to work on including the sounds of words to meet my emotional purpose.

Creation of New Activities or Tests

Within this formative assessment approach, you may be concerned about having to create new tests or exercises to verify that the students have learned. You may be able to make minimal changes to create an alternative test or exercise. Once your students have shown you their improvement since the first learning experience, you will have to provide an opportunity to verify that growth. In math, the students do the same three additional digit math problems but with different numbers. In science, a variable can be changed. In English, the students write a new comparison essay for a different theme on the same novel. In social studies students can be asked to compare the same two countries with different categories; the first time they compare the countries for geography and political stability, the second time they compare the countries for economic stability and ethnic diversity. An art teacher can have the students contrast two new paintings but have the paintings still represent the same styles as the original exercise. When the activity's level of thinking is at the higher levels of thinking, you can more easily provide different variations on the exercise with minimal effort.

Summary

- After you have observed students' work, diagnosed their learning status, offered feedback, and provided time for improvement, you want to see their improved learning.

- Students can demonstrate the changes in their work in many ways to verify their increasing progress toward doing proficient or above-proficient work.

- You can slightly vary higher-level thinking activities and tests to create new assessments or tests for your students.

6

Formative Assessment: Reporting, Grading, and Celebrating Students' Standards-Based Growth

Overview

- Setting the Stage
- Questions
- Introduction
- Reports on the Students' Progression through the Standards
- Formative Grading with Standards
- Inform Parents and Guardians about Standards Progress
- Learning Celebrations
- Summary

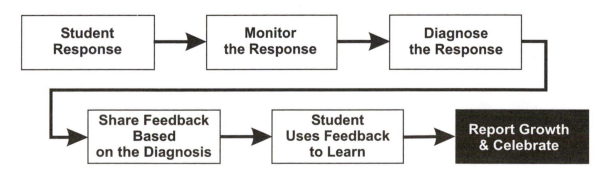

Setting the Stage

Essie watches the television for the results of last night's big basketball game. The sports announcer shows the scoring of the two rival teams through highlights of a game, and then he says, "The final score of the game is Syracuse University—60 points." Essie waits, but the announcer does not tell the score of the other team. Did Syracuse University win? Essie cannot celebrate the success of her team until she knows the score. Students and parents experience that same sense of incompletion when they do not know how the students are progressing in their learning.

Questions

♦ How do you inform your students of how they are progressing in the standards?

♦ How do you inform your students' parents or guardians of how their child is progressing in the standards?

♦ How do you grade in a formative-assessment environment?

♦ How do you celebrate the learning successes of the students?

Introduction

This chapter illustrates many ways to show the students' progress to students, parents or guardians, your team, or the administration. After you or your students have observed students in the classroom, diagnosed them, given them feedback, and given them the opportunity to implement the improvements, you also will want to celebrate their learning successes. Reporting students' standards-based progress goes beyond the daily assessments that you give the students. Your students want a global view of their learning to see how they have progressed instead of the daily microscopic view of the daily formative assessments. If students only focus on each footstep in the journey, they do not see how far they have traveled from their original starting point as indicated in Figure 6.1.

Figure 6.1. Students' Learning Journey

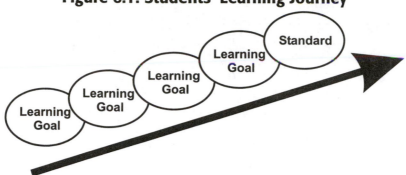

Reports on The Students' Progression through the Standards

You can use classroom standards-based assessments to inform your students on a regular basis of how well they are progressing.

Check Off Standards Milestones

For each critical goal of a standard there are many learning tasks that students need to be able to do. For example, as the English language arts department teachers, who look at the New York State Standard 3, "Language for Critical Analysis and Evaluation," you select the critical goal of "writing an analysis of ideas...using evaluative criteria from a variety of perspectives." Collectively you identify all the many learning tasks and skills milestones for this standard goal and distribute the list to the students. As students demonstrate each skill, they check it off so that they monitor their progress within the one critical goal. You list the skills down their paper.

In Sarah's success list, she puts a plus sign (+) to indicate she has demonstrated it and a blank to indicate that she has not demonstrated it thus far:

- \+   Brainstorm a main idea or theme that two pieces of literature have in common
- \+   Find supporting evidence from the various pieces of literature
- \+   Organize the evidence
- \+   Write a topical sentence that focuses on the same idea seen from two different perspectives
- \+   Decide which format to use for the paragraph (contrast sentence by sentence for both pieces of literature or contrast by all one piece of literature then all of the other
- ____   Use contrast words to emphasize the differences
- ____   Verify that the evidence from each piece of literature provides a high degree of difference to prove the contrast
- ____   Evaluate the paragraph against a standards-based rubric

Show Whole-Class Learning Successes

As you tell the students what the purpose (the critical goal of the standard), is for the lesson and list what they will be able to do as a result of the lesson, you have created a dynamic sequential classroom formative assessment to show success over time. As students are able to do each observable and measurable learning task in the list, they feel successful. You have scaffolded the learning tasks so that all students climb up the ladder of the standard from merely learning the definition of a term such as "life cycle," to applying the life cycle to an insect such as a butterfly, to creating a story about the life of a butterfly (Clarke, 2005). As all the class successfully performs the task, you can put a letter such as "S" for success in front of it as shown in Figure 6.2. When you use word processing or Power Point to list the learning tasks, you can easily add the letter in front of the successfully completed task, and you have a digital record of the successes of the class. With each learning task that all students accomplish, you and they can see their growth in that particular goal of the standard. Before the end of class, review with the students their daily progress on the critical goal of the standard. You can print out this list, display it on the class bulletin board, and refer to those successes as you start the next phase of the unit. In addition, you can post this performance list to a class website or blog.

Figure 6.2. Class Learning Success Chart

Standard 3.3		
The learner will conduct investigations and build an understanding of animal life cycles.		
Goal	**Success**	**Date**
Define life cycle	S	April 3
Label the parts of a life cycle given the cycle	S	April 3
Compare the life cycles of two different animals	S	April 5
Make up a story to illustrate the life cycle by pretending to be a specific animal		
Evaluate what stage of the life cycle a given animal is in		

Demonstrate Weekly Class Average on a Standard

Through the use of a class graph on the standard, you can share with the class their progress over time. If one of your critical aspects of your school's goals is for your students to develop writing fluency, you can show the students the entire class's progress through a graph of each week's average score (Figure 6.3). After students write for a certain number of minutes, count their total words, and show you their data, you enter that information into your PDA or tablet computer. You project the graph to show the students the average class score for that day without showing an individual scores, and talk about how the class has increased from the last observed time.

Figure 6.3. Class Standard Success Overtime

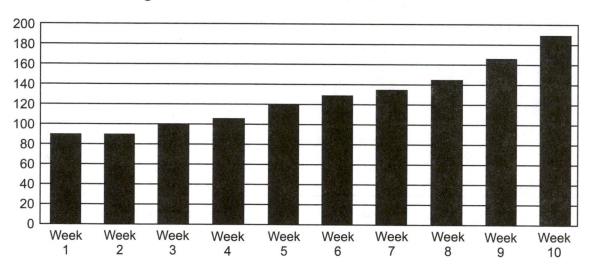

Post Individual Exemplars

As students have more of their work posted on the exemplar wall, they feel a sense of accomplishment. While your music class works on the national music standard of "Listening to, analyzing, and describing music," they have many opportunities to show exemplary work. For example, they can use the music vocabulary they have been practicing to do a concept map of the similarities between the two musical pieces. You put a plus sign (+) on top of the paper of those students who demonstrate above-proficient work, and you ask them to put their papers on the exemplar wall for this unit. For each learning experience within this standard, you post all the exemplar work such as this musical analysis in Figure 6.4.

Figure 6.4. Student Music Exemplar

Name:		
	First Piece	**Second Piece**
Melody	Lyrical	Lyrical
Instrumentation	Uses a guitar	Uses a guitar and a flute
Tension	Builds up toward end	Not as much tension as an interplay of sounds
Variety	The melody is repeated with periods of silence	The melody is repeated with a single tone connecting the repetitions

Self-Analysis of Their Own Weekly Scores

You can have students analyze their own scores on a weekly basis to see their progress (Wiggins, 1998). If you give a vocabulary quiz each week in social studies, you can have the students graph their scores in a computer spreadsheet on their laptop or in the computer lab. You can create the spreadsheet template for them and distribute it to their laptops or lab computer stations. You may give the quiz on Friday, and then on Monday you return the quiz. The students enter the score for that quiz, and the computer generates the graph (Figure 6.5). If the students score above an 80, they can continue with their present vocabulary strategy. If they score below an 80, then they can select from a list of alternative vocabulary learning strategies. They try that strategy out for the next two weeks to see if their weekly scores increase. Students tend to react to the visual impact of a graph much more than just a list of numbers. Because you have also entered their scores in your grade book or spreadsheet, you can ask students who scored below 80 what new strategy they are going to use.

Figure 6.5. Student Growth Through Spreadsheet Graph

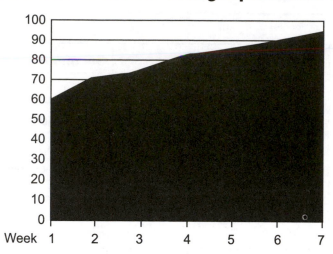

Include Present and Past Standard Scores

Another way to help your students to see their progress in a standard is to put the standards rating for this assessment and for previous assessments on the same standard on the students' paper. For example, this time Luisa scored a 5/6 and last time she scored a 4/6 on the analysis of a historical document (document-based question [DBQ]). The students, like Luisa, examine the difference between the two scores to see their growth in the standard after receiving and implementing your feedback on the last DBQ. If you include an analytic rubric or a rating scale, then the students can see exactly the areas that they have grown in. Likewise, students can put their scores in their own electronic learning logs. You may decide to show them all of their past scores for this standard:

Luisa Torres

DBQ Analysis (Standard 3.1)

This time   5/6

April 29   4/6

April 14   4/6

April 1   3/6

Document the Standard, Critical Part, or Standards-Based Rubric

As you return the students' graded assignment, you can include the actual standard, a list of the critical goals of the standard, or the rubric that is based on the standard and indicate what changes have taken place since the last time the students were assessed. You may bold the critical part of the standard that the student completed and indicate the major thinking verb such as "evaluate." You may italicize the area that still needs improvement. You can write a comment about how well the student demonstrated the standard and give some specific suggestions about how to do better next time. If you have used a standards-based rubric that uses precise standards terms as your assessment, you can use two different colors, one to indicate the positives and the other to indicate the needed changes. As illustrated in Figure 6.6, a fifth-grade California math teacher indicates different levels of proficiency based on the students' demonstrated learning. She uses an arrow to show the movement from Below Basic to Basic:

Figure 6.6. Document Standard Growth and Gaps

Quarter 1 Assessment				
	Below Basic	**Basic**	**Proficient**	**Advanced**
	→	X		
2.1	Unable to estimate, round, and manipulate very large numbers (in thousands and above) and very small numbers (thousandths and smaller)	Half of the time **estimates, rounds,** and *manipulates* **very large numbers** and *very small numbers*	Can estimate, round, and manipulate very large numbers and very small numbers	Applies estimation, rounding, and manipulation to house construction
Comment: You have mastered estimates and rounding for large numbers. Great progress! Let's try the program Max's Magnificent Math to help you with manipulating the small numbers.				

Repeat Peer Review through Assessment Tools

If peers assess each other's work throughout a project by using rubrics, then students can comprehend their progress in the critical aspect of the rubric. Students in middle school technology education may do peer review at critical parts of the standards-based project such as the planning phase, the building phase, the testing phase, and the assessment phase. The students can store these sheets in a physical binder or electronically on the network server so that they have access to all the reviews. The students "hand in" the final project along with all the rubric sheets so that you can quickly review the student's growth in the standard. Art students can also do a peer-review as indicated in Figure 6.7.

Peer Review

Figure 6.7. Repeated Peer Review

Compare				
Picasso's *Guernica* with West's *The Death of General Wolfe* in terms of depicting war.				
Standard	**Critical Goal**	**Date**	**Rating out of 8**	**Comments Based on Rubric**
Art evaluation	Analyze how two paintings treat the same topic	May 1	5 out of 8	You tell the strategies that each artist used in the painting and what aspect of war each depicts. You can improve by telling what emotion each painting conveys and giving details to support your idea. (Rubric items 5 and 6)
Art evaluation	Analyze how two paintings treat the same topic	May 8	8 out of 8	Now you use the emotional appeal of each painting as your central point. You clearly show how the artists use different strategies to present two very different views on war. Good improvement.

Display Classroom Standards Chart for Student's Progress

To have the big view of students' progress in the standards, you may want to keep a standards chart with the critical goals of the standard listed. You can create a digital spreadsheet or word-processed chart in which the student's name is on the left going down the spreadsheet, and the proficiencies go across the spreadsheet. You print out the initial spreadsheet and give it to the student. Whenever a student has successfully demonstrated a critical aspect of a particular standard for three different assignments, the student or you put a plus sign (+) or a number 1 in the spreadsheet. When you use the number 1, the computer can calculate quickly how many 1s each student has and how many students scored a 1 on this particular standard. You will want to make a spreadsheet version for yourself so that you can be aware of the progress of all students.

Your English language arts (ELA) team has decided to concentrate on specific goals within the standards and have labeled each goal with a letter, so ELA standard 1 may have four goals 1-A, 1-B, 1-C, and 1-D. You use that goal chart, put in your students' names, and indicate which learning goals each student has achieved so far as shown in Figure 6.8.

Figure 6.8. Students' Standards Progress Chart

Standard	1-A	1-B	1-C	2-A	2-B	2-C	3-A	3-B	3-C	4-A	Total
Abel, Asa	1	1		1						1	4
Bond, Bob	1										
Canton, Chris	1	1		1						1	
Dominguez, Don	1			1							
Edison, Edward	1	1		1							
Total	5	3	0	4	0	0	0	0	0	2	14

A variation is to have a Classroom Standards Progress Chart, which represents the class. A "+" or a "1" is put in a column when all the students have demonstrated that goal to the expressed high level (Figure 6.9).

Figure 6.9. Classroom Standards Progress Chart

Standard	1-A	1-B	1-C	2-A	2-B	2-C	3-A	3-B	3-C	4-A
Class	+	+								+

Show Their Own Standards Improvement

Your students can keep track of their own standards progress by putting the information into a paper chart or a digital chart. They write down what they will concretely do to improve the next time. They can electronically store these learning reflections each time they receive a graded assignment. You can look at the students' sheets and see how they can help the students to improve. Each student's submission is a cumulative submission so that both you and the students can see what strategy for improvement was proposed and if that strategy resulted in progress in the standard as depicted in Figure 6.10.

Figure 6.10. Students' Own Standard Improvements

Standard	Critical Aspect	Assignment	Date	Rating	Growth and Improvement
1.1	Listen & write	Listen to news and write a persuasive essay	May 19	3/6	◆ I will take more notes as I listen. ◆ I will label each note with a P for major point and an E for example so I can figure out what is important in my notes.
1.1	Listen & write	Listen to a speech and write a persuasive essay	May 23	4/6	I now can identify the critical parts of the passage. ◆ I will only select examples that prove my point in the essay. ◆ I will focus on proving the topic, not on including all the information.

Formative Grading with Standards

Most schools need to translate standards reporting into a traditional grading system. A critical question in grading in a formative-assessment approach is, "How do you factor in revised now-proficient or above-proficient work into grading?" You may take the revised-work grade as the sole grade for the assignment (Butler & Munn, 2006), or you may suggest a weighted grading, in which the first assignment receives a much lower weight than the revised work Reeves (2004).

Likewise, you may find that you are giving higher grades than you have in previous years. If your goal is for all students to succeed in the standards, and they do succeed, then you will have higher grades than in the past. If your school does not use a proficient grading, such as 4 = Above Proficient, 3 = Proficient, 2 = Progressing, 1 = Starting, then you will have to decide what number grade equals proficiency, such as 85 out of 100, and what number grade represents above proficiency, such as 100. If your students reach proficiency in each of the goals within the standard, then their grades will be at least 85 or B+.

As you analyze the progress of the students in their formative assessment journey, you may want to think about your grading philosophy. Because formative assessment promotes the proficient success of all students, then you might consider how your grading system reflects their "success over time" philosophy. You may find that you will adapt new grading procedures.

Use Only Proficiency Grading

You may choose to give only one of three ratings, a plus sign (+) or a 4 for above-proficient work, a checkmark (✓) or a 3 for proficient work, and comments for any work that is less than proficient. Students receive a "grade" when they receive the proficient level or higher. If your school does not use a 4–3–2–1 rating scale to assess standards progress, then you will convert your proficiency scoring into numbers. You may determine that a proficient grade is 85, whereas an above-proficient grade is 100. The students can quickly assess their progress in the course by the ratings on their papers over time.

Weight Grades

A problem in grading occurs when all grades have the same weight even though they represent very different levels of achievement within the same learning goal. Formative grading is based on students being successful in their learning. For example, Jamie, a student in your speaking course may get 60 on his first information speech, 70 on one in the middle of the course, and then at the end he earns 100 on an information speech. Jamie's grade average is 60 + 70 + 100, which is 230 divided by the 3 speeches for an average of 76. You can transform the grading by weighting the grades. Grades from the beginning of the project get a 10% weighting, the middle get 30%, and the ending ones get 60%. Therefore, a grade of 60 (beginning), 70 (middle), and 100 (ending) results in a 90, rather than the average (all scores divided by the number of assignments) of 76. Weighted scoring values the learning that has taken place over time. You can apply this grading process to Bloom's level of thinking skills with knowledge-comprehension thinking getting 10%, application-analysis getting 30%, and synthesis-evaluation getting 60% (Bloom, 1956).

Provide Five-Week Standards "Grading" Reports

At least every five weeks you should report to students their academic success by giving them a report from your standards-based spreadsheet or grading program. You can give paper copies or have students access their grades on line. Your grading program or spreadsheet will be based on the standards (Marzano, 2000). Instead of the normal headings of tests, homework, project, you use the standards such as Standard 1, Standard 2, and so forth. When you record an assignment grade, you list it under the appropriate critical goal of the standard. For example, you no longer record a listening comprehension test under the category of "test," but you do record it under "Standard 1: Understanding," because the test measures student progress in ability to listen and understand oral speech. Label it as "S1 Listening" to illustrate that it is Standard 1, and the specific task is listening. The students will receive the same grades, but their grades will be averaged under each standard so that the students and parents can see how well the students are doing in terms of the standard (see below). A 55 in a Standard 3 category has more meaning than a 55 in a testing category. The only caveat is that each assignment, homework, and project has to be directly related to a critical aspect of a standard. There are classroom management systems that can be used to track students' progress on standards.

Usual Grading Categories

Part Note taking	Sept. 10	70	
Quiz Literary Terms	Sept. 12	50	
Part Listening	Sept. 15	80	Quiz Average = 60
Test Theme	Oct. 3	60	Participation Average = 78
Quiz Web	Oct. 6	75	Test Average = 55
Test Poem Novel Compare	Nov. 10	50	Grade = 64
Part Chart	Nov. 12	75	
Quiz Three Themes	Nov. 17	55	

Standards-Based Grading

S1 Note taking	Sept. 10	70	
S1 Listening	Sept. 15	80	
S1 Web	Oct. 6	75	S1 Average = 75
S1 Chart	Nov. 12	75	S2 Average = 54

S2 Literary Terms	Sept. 12	50	S3 Average = 55
S2 Theme	Oct. 3	60	Grade: 64
S2 Poem Novel Compare	Nov. 10	50	
S3 Three Themes	Nov. 17	55	

Grade with Standards Comments

Instead of just a letter or number grade to represent the students' learning, add comments on which standards or goals within the standard have been met, and which have not been met at this time. Most report card systems have a number code for teachers' comments. With the help of your team, you can create a list of the key goals of the standards. Your team will probably already have a word-processed list you can use. The new report card might look like Figure 6.11.

Figure 6.11. Report Grade, Standard, and Feedback

Social Studies					
Student	**Grade**	**Standard**	**Mastered**	**Not Mastered Yet**	**Comment**
Wanda Wallis	C	4. Economics	✓Key Terms ✓Natural Resources	◆ Monetary system ◆ Capital resources and human resources ◆ Cost-Benefit Analysis ◆ Investments ◆ Banking	Wanda, you can use the online "Money and Me" or do the online banking simulation to make additional progress.

Provide Standards-Based Report Cards

Another way to report student progress is through a standards-based report card. The San Francisco Unified School District has a report card in which the skills are listed, and the teachers record the student's status by using the scale of 4 = above proficiency; 3 = proficient; 2 = basic; 1 = below basic; scale; or not assessed (San Francisco Unified School District, 2007). A sample of the fifth-grade report card section (Figure 6.12) illustrates how the students receive their quarterly rating in science.

Figure 6.12. Standard-Based Report Card

Science		Q1	Q2	Q3	Q4
1.0	Understands that matter is composed of elements and their combinations				
2.0	Understands that organisms have structures for respiration, digestion, waste disposal, and transport of materials				
3.0	Understands that water moves between oceans and the land through evaporation and condensation				

Have Quarterly Individual Student Meetings

In addition to simply giving the students their standards "report card," you can schedule quarterly meetings (the end of each 10 weeks) with your students to go over their standards progress. You can have the students talk about how they are progressing in each standard and what things they have been successful in. You can ask them what they can do to improve in the standards. Based on their analysis of their areas for improvement and your data on their progress for each critical aspect, you suggest specific activities to help them in their progress in that standard. If you feel that you do not have time for these quarterly meetings, consider the amount of time you spend in preparing for state benchmarks or state exams. If you already spend six days in getting the students ready for the state tests, you could use those six days for student quarterly meetings instead.

Students' Questions to Prepare for the Quarterly Meeting

The following is a list of questions students might use during their quarterly meetings (Cummings, 2000).

- ♦ What standards or critical aspects of the standards do I feel I am doing well in?
- ♦ What evidence do I have?
- ♦ What standards or critical aspects of the standards have I have not yet started?
- ♦ What standards or critical aspects of the standards do I feel I need improvement in?
- ♦ What evidence do I have?

♦ What suggestions do I have for my own improvement?

♦ A final category that students will complete after talking with the teacher is, "What I will do in the next five weeks to improve in the standards." (p. 28)

Test Periodically on the Standards

Your school district may have periodic testing on the standards through the year on a regular basis such as every six weeks in which all standards are tested each time. Commercial programs such as Acuity provide these benchmarks in math and language. A digital report on the progress of your students on each standard is generated, and you can give each student this information. A sample chart is shown in Figure 6.13. Their progress in your course should not be a mystery to the students or their parents.

Figure 6.13. Periodic Standard Testing

Math 8 Cycle 1 Sept.													
Name	1.1	1.2	1.3	2.1	2.2	2.3	2.4	3.1	3.2	3.3	3.4	3.5	4.1	4.2
Cooper, Marg	1	1		1				1	1					1

Build in Electronic Portfolios

As you build frequent electronic portfolio review days into your schedule, you permit your students to self-assess themselves in their standards progress. Approximately every five weeks, they are asked to select the example of their work that best shows how they have achieved the critical goal. They look at all their examples in terms of the critical aspect. They may pick their lab report on purifying stream water to be like tap water during the first five weeks as their best example. They write a reflection on what they have learned about the critical standard aspect through this stream lab. During the next five weeks, they will compare all of their recent other lab reports to the stream lab report to select the one that best exemplifies their success in the standard (see below). Your students can do mini-portfolio presentations in which they show you their growth in the standard. At the end of the year, you may choose to use the electronic portfolio as the class final in which your students demonstrate their progress toward the standards with their own examples and reflections.

> I have decided to replace my purifying water lab report with my stream lab report. In the stream report, my team created its own research question, designed the experiment, analyzed the results, and rejected the hypothesis through a long explanation, and explained the implications. We did the work ourselves in the purifying water lab. Mr. Bender gave us the experiment and the structured lab report form.

Inform Parents and Guardians about Standards Progress

Not only do students want to know their progress, but their parents or guardians also want to know their progress on a regular basis.

Have Parents Assess their Child's Learning

If you frequently involve the parents and/or guardians of your students in assessing their children's standard-based work according to a checklist, rubric, or rating, then they know the progress of their children for the specific standard. They can report back to you on the successes of their children and the areas for additional work. For the parents to be able to assess their children, the assessment tool has to be very clear in both the content and the quality required.

Provide Web-Based Standards Grading

Parents can access a web-based class grading program such as Blackboard to see how the students are progressing in the standards as long as the grading program has been changed to have standards based categories as shown in Figure 6.14. If they have access to a usual online grading program, which uses the categories of "test," "homework," and "projects," then they will not learn how well the students are doing in the standards. If you do not have a web-based grading program, then email them a printout from your standards-based grading program or spreadsheet.

Figure 6.14. Web-Based Satndards Grading

Grade: 64

Standard 1 Average = 75

S1 Note taking	Sept 10	70
S1 Listening	Sept. 15	80
S1 Web	Oct. 6	75
S1 Chart	Nov. 12	75

Standard 2 Average = 54

S2 Lit Terms	Sept. 12	50
S2 Theme	Oct. 3	60
S2 Poem/Novel Compare	Nove. 10	50

Satndrd 3 Average = 55

S3 Three Themes	Nov. 17	55

Have Parent Conferences

Likewise, parent conferences can focus on the progress of the students in the standards instead of talking about the student's work in general terms such as "Huan is doing average." When parents hear "Huan has shown increasing improvement in his math in representing and comparing whole numbers and decimals. He has shown his improvement through...," they have something definite to feel proud of or to ask questions about. This new version of a parent conference is to walk, verbally and visually, the parents through the grade level's expected standards and let the parents know where their children are in each standard. The students are not compared to one another, but they are compared to their own progress on the standards. Another even more powerful version of the parent conference is for the students to lead the conference. They show their parents their progress on each standard through organized examples of their work, such as a physical or electronic portfolio.

Provide a Standards Chart

You can mail or e-mail the parents the standards chart to depict the student's progress in the standards. When the parents can see all of the critical goals of each standard, they realize the academic responsibility of their child. Parents can easily see all the goals of the standards for which the student is responsible, a listing of the present standards such as 1-A, 1-B, and can see which ones the student has already achieved. Also, they realize the other critical goals in which the student has not yet reached a level of proficiency.

Figure 6.15 shows only those goals for which the class is presently responsible for learning. A plus indicates successful completion and a dash indicates no successful completion to date.

Figure 6.15. Partial Standards Chart for Parents

Standard	1-A	1-B		2-A				3-C	4-A
Abel, Abigail	+	+		+				--	+

Figure 6.16 shows the parents all the goals but includes a slash to indicate that certain goals have not yet been taught in class.

Figure 6.16. Complete Standards Chart for Parents

Standard	1-A	1-B	1-C	2-A	2-B	3-A	3-B	3-C	4-A
Abel, Abigail	+	+	/	+	/	/	/	--	+

Include Standards
Results in a Newsletter

Tell of the achievements of the class by physically giving the students a paper newsletter to take home or by virtually distributing a newsletter through e-mail, the class website, or the class blog. Include information on the key standards' goals on which all students have been successful. Indicate those key goals which have been introduced and not yet mastered by all students. The report can include a list of the learning tasks that all students have accomplished. Do not focus the newsletter on the "cute" things that have happened in the classroom or on what textbook chapters have been covered, but focus on how well all the students are progressing toward the standard. For your elementary science class, for example, you may indicate that the class is learning that weather changes from day to day and over the seasons; the students can all describe the weather by temperature, wind direction and speed, and precipitation. They are working on identifying the weather for each season. You can showcase exemplary student work for each goal. You can include suggestions for the parents to help their children in learning the standard.

Learning Celebrations

As you and your students see their learning over time and see this learning represented in some score reporting system, you and they have many opportunities to celebrate successes.

Get Short Wins
for Long-Range Success

Because both a standards-based approach and a formative assessment approach focus on students' successes, then students, parents, teachers, and administrators have many opportunities to celebrate successes as the students progress through the standards. Schmoker (2006, pp. 122–123) emphasizes the importance of short-term wins with Hamel's "win small, win early, win often," and Collins's "steady stream of successes." When students feel successful, they are motivated to learn. When you break the learning into meaningful blocks and formatively assess on those blocks, students can see their small wins.

If your team administers the same assessment and collaboratively scores it on at least a monthly basis, then your team has valuable information on student progress to report to students, parents, and administration. They have reason for a joyous celebration about student successes (Reeves, 2004).

Celebrate Learning Success for Individuals and the Class

Figure 6.17 indicates many ways to celebrate learning successes for the individual and for the class.

Figure 6.17. Celebrate Individual and Class Learning Success

Celebrate Individual Student's Successes	Celebrate Class Successes
✓ Success in performing a specific standards-based learning task	✓ Success in performing a specific standards-based learning task
✓ Growth in a series of tasks that successfully demonstrates one category of a learning goal within a standard	✓ Growth in a series of tasks that successfully demonstrates one category of a learning goal within a standard
✓ Cumulative success in a series of tasks that demonstrates the comprehensive nature of one learning goal within a standard	✓ Growth in a series of tasks that successfully demonstrates part of the learning goal within a standard.
✓ Demonstration of all the selected goals in a standard	✓ Exemplary work produced by the class as a whole
✓ Improvement in one of his or her own goals	✓ Cumulative success in a series of tasks that demonstrates the comprehensive nature of one learning goal within a standard
✓ Accomplishment of one of his or her own goals	✓ Demonstration of all the selected goals in a standard
✓ Improvement in several of his or her own goals	
✓ Achievement of proficient work	
✓ Exemplary work	

Hold Student Learning Celebrations

There are many ways to celebrate that reward student learning. Students can

◆ Show their own graph of their learning, either in skills, goals, or standards achieved from the beginning of the year to now. For example, your elementary math student, Nika, produces a graph of the tasks within the "evaluate reasonableness of solutions" goal for mathematical reasoning to show all of the tasks that she has now completed.

- Showcase their beginning and their to-date work to highlight their improvements. For example, a high school science student, Maria, shows her original concept map about the stream environment and her most recent one that reveals drastically more categories and more connections among the categories.

- Present a electronic portfolio that demonstrates the various changes in their understanding of the expectations through their selection of items and their reflections. For example, Magnus shows his art sculpture and explains the changes he went through as he thought about his project and worked with the clay to create his sculpture. He used digital photographs and iPod recorded digital commentary to document his changes. He included several clips of his teacher, Mr. Airasian, giving him feedback.

- Create posters to highlight growth. For example, Jacob made a list of the Mandarin communication topics that he now can speak about. He included such topics as: restaurant, bank, post office, interview, travel, hospital, and house. At the beginning of this high school year, he could not speak on any of these topics; now he can speak fluently within these topics. He includes various ways, such as peer feedback and teacher feedback, that helped him to speak within those topics

- Copy sections from their digital learning journal to demonstrate their changes in thinking. For example, Jonas copies sections from his journal to show his changes in thinking about building a toothpick bridge as he plans, builds, and tests out the bridge, then plans again, builds again, and tests it out again in his middle school technology class.

- Put their exemplar on the classroom wall once they and you have agreed it is exemplary work. For example, Lea's illustration of the water cycle clearly indicates her understanding of evaporation and condensation; as her middle school science teacher, you ask her to put her illustration under the water goal on the wall of fame.

- Show their metaphorical learning road in which they fill in each goal brick that they have completed so that they can see how far they have traveled on their learning road. The box are really just little boxes or squares from a spreadsheet.

- Present at parent-teacher-student conference. For example, Chloe, an elementary social studies student, takes her parents through each goal and shows evidence of her work. She shows her iMovie to demonstrate her understanding of community to them. Chloe shows an initial drawing she had done of "community" and the changes she has made based on your feedback.

- Present at learning fairs, parent teas, or community-showcase sessions. For example, Enzo, an elementary English as other language student, shows an iMovie he made to introduce the school to a new student. His iMovie includes all the daily things that a student does at the school such as using a locker and walking in the halls.

- Give classroom testimonials. All of the students can proudly proclaim in which learning task or goal they have done proficient work. For example, Mrs. Mosteller ends her middle school music class with classroom learning testimonials. One of her students starts off with, "I am Lucia, and I am a successful learner. I can demonstrate the difference between beat and rhythm. Listen..."

Celebrate Class Successes

Many of the celebrations listed in the previous section can be used for the whole class. In addition, you can:

- Verbally congratulate the whole class on their daily successes. For example, Miss Yatkin starts off her class with a list of the math learning goals for the present standard. For every goal that the students have achieved, she loudly says, "Yes!," and some days, has the students say "Yes"!

- Showcase work on the class website, blog, print newsletter, or on the wall outside your room. Tell about the standard, its goals, and then show students' work that demonstrates the goals.

- Have your students applaud or pat themselves on the back when the whole class has shown improvement. For example, when all the students in Ms. Bodone's elementary science classroom have demonstrated that they can identify the differences in three plants, she asks the class to applaud themselves.

- Show Power Point presentations or iMovies of stages of the work from the beginning to the completed complex task. Emphasize the various skills, tasks, or goals that the students used.

- Show the class a graph of their starting point and their present progress in a specific learning goal.

- Select a sound clip such as horn blowing to announce success. Whenever all students have demonstrated proficiency in a goal, you announce the goal and "toot" their success.

- Have a class thermometer to show the learning over time for a particular standard. For example, Ms. Fontana has a large thermometer drawing that represents all the learning tasks within one goal. As all of the class successfully completes a task, she fills in that part of the thermometer. The class can see their success in very measurable terms. A variation is to have a growing list of the goals that the whole class has achieved.

Summary

♦ After students have used the formative assessment cycle, they have grown into a proficient or above-proficient learning for the standard. There are numerous ways for them to see their success that has taken place over time.

♦ As you use formative assessment, you will think more about how your grading system might better reflect the success model of formative assessment. Your grading can reflect their proficiency-based learning.

♦ You can demonstrate the students' standards-based learning successes in many ways to parents or guardians.

♦ As your students show success at many different parts of the learning, you and they can celebrate these successes.

References

Afflerback, P. (2005). National Reading Conference Policy Brief: High Stakes Testing and Reading Assessment. *Journal of Literacy Research, 37*(2), 151–162

Ainsworth, L., & Viegut, D. (2006). *Common formative assessments.* Thousand Oaks, CA: Corwin Press.

Alaska Department of Education & Early Development. (1996). *A collection of assessment strategies.* Retrieved February 14, 2007, from http://www.eed.state.ak.us/tls/Frameworks/mathsci/ms5_2as1.htm

Angelo, T. A., & Cross, P. K. (1993). *Classroom assessment techniques* (2nd ed.). San Francisco: Jossey-Bass.

Arizona Department of Education. (2007). *Formative assessment.* Retrieved November 22, 2007, from https://www.ideal.azed.gov/node

Atkin, J. M., & Coffey, J. E. (2003). *Everyday assessment in the science classroom.* Arlington, VA: National Science Teachers Press.

Black, P., Harrison, C., Lee, C., Marshall, B., & Wiliam, D. (2002). *Working inside the black box.* London: King's College London School of Education.

Black, P., & Wiliam, D. (1998). Inside the black box: Raising standards through classroom assessment [Electronic version]. *Phi Delta Kappan, 80* (2), 139–148. Retrieved July 30, 2005, from http://www.pdkintl.org/kappan/kbla9810.htm

Bloom B. S. (1956). *Taxonomy of Educational Objectives, Handbook I: The Cognitive Domain.* New York: David McKay Co Inc.

British Columbia Ministry of Education. (1997). *Managing assessment instrumentation.* Retrieved December 8, 2007, from http://www.bced.gov.bc.ca/irp/mathk7/appdmai.htm

British Columbia Ministry of Education. (2007). *Managing assessment instrumentation.* Retrieved December 8, 2007, from http://www.bced.gov.bc.ca/irp/mathk7/appdmai.htm

Brown, E., Gibbs, G., & Glover, C. (2003). Evaluation tools for investigating the impact of assessment regimes on student learning: Appendix 1: Assessment review checklist.BEE-j 2. Retrieved December 28, 2007, from www.bioscience.heacademy.ac.uk/journal/v012/beej-2–5apx.pdf

Brown, G., & Irby, B. J. (2001). *The principal portfolio* (3rd ed.). Thousand Oaks, CA: Corwin Press.

Butler, R. (1988). Enhancing and undermining intrinsic motivation. *British Journal of Educational Psychology, 58,*1–14.

Butler, S. M., & Munn, N. D. (2006). *A teacher's guide to classroom assessment*. San Francisco: Jossey-Bass.

California State Board of Education. (2007). *Visual and performing arts: Visual arts content standards*. Retrieved December 14, 200, from http://www.cde.ca.gov/be/st/ss/vagrade7.asp

Calkins, L. M. (1986). *Art of teaching writing*. Portsmouth, NH: Heinemann.

Carless, D. (2003). *Learning-oriented assessment.*Paper presented at the Evaluation and Assessment Conference Adelaide, University of South Australia, November 25, 2003.

Carr, J. F., & Harris, D. E. (2001). *Succeeding with standards linking curriculum, assessment, and action planning*. Alexandria, VA: Association for Supervision and Curriculum Development.

Chapin, S. H., O'Connor, C., & Anderson, N. C. (2003). *Classroom discussions: Using math talk to help students learn*. Sausalito, CA: Math Solutions Publications.

Chin, C. (2006). Classroom interaction in science: Teacher questioning and feedback to students' responses. *International Journal of Science Education, 28* (11), 1315–1346.

Clarke, S. (2005). *Enriching feedback in the primary classroom*. London: Hodder-Murray.

Clarke, S. (2007). *Formative assessment in action: Weaving the elements together*. London: Hodder-Murray.

Committee on Undergraduate Science Education. (1997). *Science teaching reconsidered: A handbook*. Washington, DC: National Academy Press. Retrieved November 9, 2007, from http://www.nap.edu/readingroom/books/str/4.html

Cotton, K. (1988). *Monitoring student learning in the classroom*. Northwest Regional Educational Laboratory. Retrieved August 14, 2008, from http://www.nwrel.org/scpd/sirs/2/cu4.html

Covey, Stephen. (1990). *The 7 habits of highly effective people*. Old Tappan, NJ: Free Press.

Cowie, B., & Bell, B. (1999). A model of formative assessment in science education. *Assessment in Education, 6*(1), 102–116.

Cummings, C. (2000). *Winning strategies for classroom management*. Alexandria, VA: Association for Supervision and Curriculum Development.

Erickson, F. (2007). Some thoughts on "proximal" formative assessments of student learning. In P. Moss (Ed.), *Evidence and decision making* (pp. 186–216). Malden, MA: Blackwell.

Erwin, J. C. (2004). *The classroom of choice: Giving students what they need and getting what you want*. Alexandria, VA: Association for Supervision and Curriculum Development.

Georgia Department of Education. (2006). *Seventh-grade science curriculum.* Retrieved November 22, 2007, from http://www.georgiastandards.org/DMGetDocument.aspx/Seventh%20Grade%20Revised%2006.pdf?p=6CC6799F8C1371F657C21D1A32498DDE75FCCCF994A9AB550E478FD0D28F91C4&Type=D

Greater Saskatoon Catholic Schools. (n.d.). *Teacher assistant handbook: Appendix D: Student observation and recording.* Retrieved November 2, 2007, from http://www.scs.sk.ca/instructional_services/ta/appendixd.asp.

Hall, K., & Burke, W. M. (2003). *Making formative assessment work: Effective practice in the primary classroom.* Berkshire, England: Open University Press.

Hammond, M. J. (2002). *Feedback on assessment: Developing a practitioner handbook.* Education-line. Retrieved March 2, 2007, from http://www.leeds.ac.uk/educol/documents/00002125.htm

Hattie, J. (1999, August). *Influences on student learning.* Inaugural lecture: Professor of Education, University of Auckland.

Hattie, J. & Jaeger, R. (1998). Assessment and classroom learning: A deductive approach. *Assessment in Education, 5*(1), 111–122

Hawaii Geographic Alliance. (2006). *Standards I can statements performance indicators.* Retrieved December 12, 2007, from http://hawaii.edu/hga/ASG100/window/STANDArd.pdf.

Hawk, K., & Hill, J. (2001). The challenge of formative assessment in secondary classrooms. *SPANZ Journal* (Sept.) Whitanga: Aries Publishing.

Hayes, H. H. (2004). *Getting results with curriculum mapping.* Alexandria, VA: Association for Supervision and Curriculum Development.

Heritage, M. (2007a). *Formative assessment: What teachers need to know and do.* Presentation delivered at UCLA National Center for Research on Evaluation, Standards, and Student Testing in New Orleans, Louisiana, February 3–4, 2007.

Heritage, M. (2007b). Formative assessment: What do teachers need to know and do? *Phi Delta Kappan, 89* (2), 140–145, from Academic Search Premier.

Herman, J. L., Aschbacher, P. R., & Winters, L. (1992). *A practical guide to alternative assessment.* Alexandria, VA: Association for Supervision and Curriculum Development.

Hodgen, J., & Marshall, B. (2005). Assessment for learning in English and mathematics: A comparison. *Curriculum Journal, 16* (2), 153–176.

Hounsell, D. (2003). *No comment? Reshaping feedback to foster high-quality learning.* Edinburgh: University of Edinburgh, Learning and Teaching Forum on Formative Assessment, November 27, 2003.

Hounsell, D. (2005). *Reinventing feedback in the contemporary university.* South Australian Branch of HERDSA Seminar, 1, University of Adelaide. Retrieved November 22, 2007, from http://www.adelaide.edu.au/clpd/online/resources/TenStrategies4EffectiveFeedback.pdf

Hunter, M. (1976). Teacher competency: Problem, theory, and practice. *Theory into Practice, 15*(2), pp. 162–171.

Hunter, M. (1982). *Mastery teaching*. El Segundo, CA: Tip Publication.

Idaho State Department of Education. (2007). *Mathematics content standards: Grade 6.*Retrieved December 13, 2007, from http://wwwside/idaho.gov/Content Standards/ICSGrade6math-1.doc

Jefferson Parish Public Schools. (n.d.). *Quilt stage III prompt student responses.* Retrieved November 11, 2007, from www.jppss.k12.1a.us/teachers/quilt/QUILT%20Stage%20III.ppt

Johnson, D. P. (2005). *Sustaining change in schools: How to overcome differences and focus on quality*. Alexandria, VA: Association for Supervision and Curriculum Development.

Kansas State Education Department. (n.d.). *Kansas state science standards*. Retrieved March 8, 2007, from http://www.ksde.org/Default.aspx?tabid=144

Leahy, S., Lyon, C., Thompson, M., & Wiliam, D. (2005). Classroom assessment minute by minute, day by day. *Educational Leadership, 63*(3), 19–24.

Library of Congress. (n.d.). *Image of our people teacher anecdotal record*. Retrieved November 07, 2007, from http://memory.loc.gov/ammem/ndlpedu/lessons/99/westnew/observe.html

Lipton, L., & Wellman, B. (1998). *Pathways to understanding: Patterns and practice in the learning-focused classroom*. Guilford, VT: Pathways Publishing.

Math Medics. (2007). S.O.S. Math. Retrieved November 12, 2007, from http://www. sosmath.com/index.html

Marzano, R. J. (2000). *Transforming classroom grading*. Alexandria, VA: Association for Supervision and Curriculum Development.

Marzano, R. J. (2007). *The art and science of teaching*. Alexandria, VA: Association for Supervision and Curriculum Development.

Marzano, R. J., & Pickering, D. J. (1997). *Dimensions of learning teacher's manual*(2nd ed.). Alexandria, VA: Association for Supervision and Curriculum Development.

McTighe, J., & O'Connor, K. (2006). Seven practices for effective learning. *Educational Leadership, 63* (3), 10–17.

Meier, D. (1999). *Accelerated learning course builder*[multimedia toolkit]. Lake Geneva, WI: Center for Accelerated Learning.

Mid-Continental Research for Education and Learning (MCREL). (2008). *List of benchmarks for geography*. Retrieved May 1, 2008, from http://www.mcrel.org/compendium/standardDetails.asp?subjectID= 8&standardID=6

Missouri Department of Elementary and Secondary Education. (2001). *Foreign Language Framework for Curriculum Development in Alignment with Missouri's Frameworks.* Jefferson City, MI: Missouri Department of Elementary and Secondary Education.

Namibian National Institute for Educational Development. (2003). *Questioning techniques.* Retrieved December 8, 2007, from http://www.edsnet.na/Resources/TBCM/TBCM14/page2.htm

National Business Education Association. (2001). *Business education standards—communication.* Retrieved November 10, 2007, from http://www.nbea.org/curriculum/s_commun.html

National Center for Fair and Open Testing. (2007). *Fact sheet on the value of formative assessment.* Retrieved December 14, 2007, from http://www.fairtest.org/facts/formulative_assessment.html

National Committee on Science Education Standards and Assessment, National Research Council. (1998). *National science education standards.* Retrieved December 14, 2007, from http://books.nap.edu/readingroom/books/str/4.html

Nebraska Department of Education. (2007). *Six quality criteria 2007 brush-up sessions.* Retrieved March 4, 2007, from http://www.sixqualitycriteria brushupsession2007_000.ppt

New York State Education Department. (2007). *English language arts Regents examinations comprehensive English.* Retrieved January 5, 2008, from http://www.nysedregents.org/testing/engre/regenteng.html

New York State Education Department. (n.d.). *Social studies standard 2: World history.* Retrieved December 13, 2007, from http://esmsc.nysed.gov/ciai/socst/socstandards/soc21.htm

New Zealand Council for Educational Research. (2001). Assessment Resource Banks. Retrieved January 5, 2008, from http://arb.nzcer.org.nz/nzcer3/nzcer.htm

O'Shea, M. R. (2006). *From standards to success.* Alexandria, VA: Association for Supervision and Curriculum Development.

Ohio State Department of Education. (2007). *Tools for teachers: Social studies academic content standards.* Retrieved November 10, 2007, from http://www.ode.state.oh.us/GD/Templates/Pages/ODE/ODEDetail.aspx?page=3&TopicRelationID=335&ContentID=852&Content=32668

Parrott, A.M. (n.d.). *Chapter 5 teaching skills lesson 5 graphic organizers.* Retrieved November 10, 2007, from http://www.africangreyparrott.com/files/graphic organizers.pdf

Pearson. (2007). *Formative assessment solutions from Pearson.* Retrieved November 20, 2007, from http://formative.pearsonassessments.com/benchmark

Popham, W. J. (2008). *Transformative assessment.* Alexandria, VA: Association for Supervision and Curriculum Development.

Primary National Strategy. (2004). Part 5: Feedback on learning. Retrieved November 10, 2007, from http://www.standards.dfes.gov.uk/primary/features/resources/primary/ pns_landt052104a41_s5.pdf

Project Based Learning Checklists. (2007). Retrieved November 11, 2007, from http://pblchecklist.4teachers.org/index.shtml

Reeves, D. B. (2004). *Accountability for learning how teachers and school leaders take charge.* Alexandria, VA: Association for Supervision and Curriculum Development.

Reeves, D. B. (2006). *The learning leader: How to focus school improvement for better results.* Alexandria, VA: Association for Supervision and Curriculum Development.

Reif, R. J. (2004). *Science standards, implementation and assessment.* Retrieved March 8, 2007, from www.nmlites.org/standards/documents/espanola-presentation-04–08–18.ppt

Sadler, D. R. (1998). Formative assessment: Revisiting the territory. *Assessment in Education, 5* (1), 77–84.

San Francisco Unified School District. (2007). *Fifth-grade report grade.* Retrieved November 20, 2007, from http://sfportal.sfusd.edu/sites/translation/archive/Lists/Translated%20Documents%20Archive/Attachments/49/Elementary%20Report%20Card%20Grade%205%20Draft%20August%20Revise.pdf

Schmoker, M. (2006). *Results now: How we can achieve unprecedented improvements in teaching and learning.* Alexandria, VA: Association for Supervision and Curriculum Development.

School Improvement in Maryland. (2007). *Using the VSC: Mathematics, grade K.* Retrieved December 8, 2007, from http://mdk12.0rg/instruction/prereqs/mathematics/gradeK/3B1a.html

Science Education Resource Center at Careleton College. (2008). *Teacher logistics—Peer review.* Retrieved May 1, 2008, from http://serc.carleton.edu/introgeo/peerreview/instructor.html#2

Shepard, L. (2000). The role of assessment in a learning culture. *Educational Researcher, 29*(7), 4–14.

South Carolina Education Oversight Committee. (2007). *A guide for parents and families about what your tenth grader should be learning in school this year.* Retrieved December 13, 2007, from http://www.sceoc.com/NR/rdonlyres/21A651E-db5a-498d-9232-c8de7170312/5440/EOCBrochure10th.pdf

State Education Department of Arizona. (n.d.). *Arizona standards—Foreign language standards.* Retrieved November 10, 2007, from http://seamonkey.ed.asu.edu/emc300/azstandards/flrationale.htm

Stiggins, R. J. (2002). Assessment crisis: The absence of assessment for learning. *Phi Delta Kappan, 83*(10), 758–765.

Stiggins. R. J. (2004). From formative assessment to assessment for learning: A path to success in standards-based schools. *Phi Delta Kappan, 87*(4), December 2005, 324–328.

Stiggins, R. J. (2007a). Assessment through the student's eyes. *Educational Leadership, 67* (8), 22–26.

Stiggins, R. J. (2007b). *An introduction to student-involved assessment for learning*(5th ed.). Upper Saddle River, NJ: Pearson Education.

Stronge, J. H. (2002). *Qualities of effective teachers.* Alexandria, VA: Association for Supervision and Curriculum Development.

Teachers of English to Speakers of Other Languages. (2007). *ESL standards for pre-K–12 students: Grades 9–12.* Retrieved December 28, 2007, from http://www.tesol.org/s_tesol/sec_document.asp?CID=113&DID=316

Tomlinson, C. A., & McTighe, J. (2006). *Integrating differentiated instruction + understanding by design.* Alexandria, VA: Association for Supervision and Curriculum Development.

Tunstall, P., & Gipps, C. (1996). Teacher feedback to young children in formative assessment: A typology. *British Educational Research Journal, 22* (4).

Tuttle, H. G. (2004). *Learning and technology assessments for administrators.* Ithaca, NY: Epilog Visions.

Tuttle, H. G. (2007a). Digital-age assessment. *Tech Learning, 27* (7), 22–24.

Tuttle, H. G. (2007b). Standards-based learning: Helping students achieve. *Classroom Connect Connected Learning, 14* (2), 4–6.

Tuttle, H. G. (2007c). Pre-test coverage from year long to small parts of unit. *Education with Technology.* Retrieved May 3, 2008, from http://eduwithtechn.wordpress.com/wp-admin/post.php?action=edit&post=293

Tuttle, H. G. (2007d). Every two weeks formative assessment model. *Education with Technology.* Retrieved January 8, 2008 from http://eduwithtechn.wordpress.com/2007/04/12/every-two-weeks-formative-assessment-model/.

Tuttle, H. G. (2007e). Formative embedded assessment versus pre-assessment and post-assessment. *Education with Technology.* Retrieved May 2, 2008, from http://eduwithtechn.wordpress.com/wp-admin/post.php?action=edit&post=658

Tuttle, H. G. (2007f). Diagnostic test with technology at the beginning of the school year. *Education with Technology.* Retrieved January 8, 2008, from http://eduwithtechn.wordpress.com/2007/09/12/diagnostic-test-with-technology-at-the-beginning-of-the-school-year/

Tuttle, H. G. (2007g). Checking for understanding: Coupons for more than participation in the classroom. *Education with Technology.* Retrieved January 8, 2008, from http://eduwithtechn.wordpress.com/2007/10/16/checking-for-under-standing-coupons-for-more-than-participation-in-the-classroom/

Tuttle, H. G. (2007h). Homework feedback using models/exemplars. *Education with Technology*. Retrieved January 8, 2008, from http://eduwithtechn.word press.com/2007/11/12/homework-feedback-using-modelsexemplars/.

Wiggins, G. (1998). Educative assessment: Designing assessments to inform and improve student performance. San Francisco: Jossey-Bass.

Willis, J. (2006). *Research-based strategies to ignite student learning*. Alexandria, VA: Association for Supervision and Curriculum Development.

Yee, K. (n.d.). *Interactive techniques*. Retrieved November 27, 2007, from http://www.fctl.ucf.edu/tresources/content/101_Tips.pdf